My Wild Wife
A love story, sorta

Steve Jewell

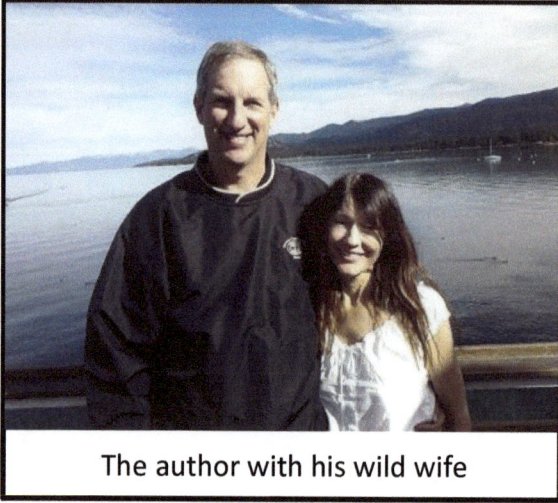

The author with his wild wife

First Edition

ISBN: 0-9981593-0-1
ISBN-13: 978-0-9981593-0-0

DEDICATION

I should dedicate this book to my wife, Shar, but the whole book is a dedication to her. Instead, I'll dedicate this to my parents, Al and Eileen and to Shar's parents Robert and Charmaine – without whom this love story would never have happened.

Contents

Introduction

This is a story about my wife Shar. It is mostly a love story - filled with tales about our life together. Nothing a 10 year old boy would cringe about, but in truth a story about an amazing woman who's also my wife.

There are many unique things about Shar. She loves all types of nature, has no fear, and frequently has ideas that are hilarious. Unfortunately, she also acts many of these out - and that's the subject of this book. She really does fascinate me. Lucille Ball made a living acting out crazy stories on TV. Shar lives this life and allows me to be Ricky Ricardo in real life. OK - She has no obsession with being on TV; but she should.

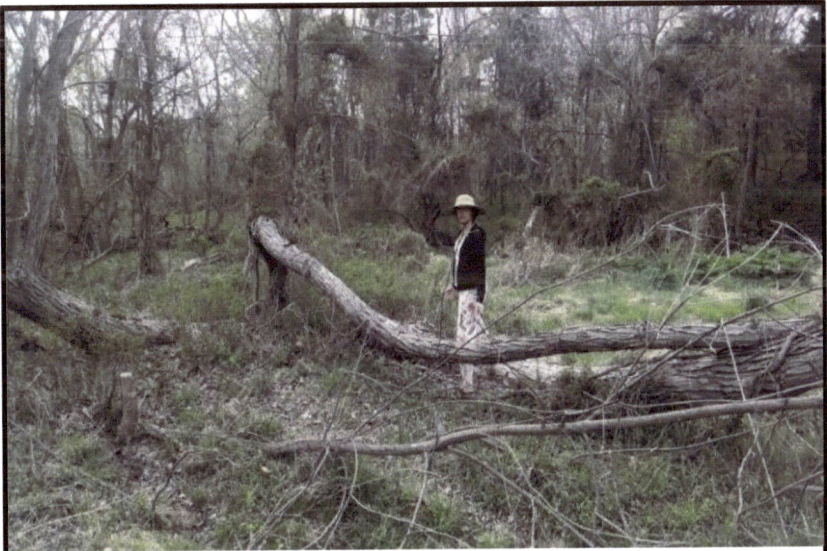

My wife Shar in her natural state – Out standing in her field

Many people love the outdoors (myself included), but she enjoys it more than anyone else I know. She will walk in the woods at any time and in any place. She's more than a little dangerous - and has no problem confronting animals with the best of the reality TV stars. She's an incredible blend of little girl, tomboy, and daredevil. To be honest, it's a bit hard to keep track of which will show up at any moment in time.

Part of her loving nature is loving animals. Many people love their pets and she does too, but she's more enthralled with animals in the wild. She loves birds, squirrels, snakes, foxes, turtles, you name it - she loves them all and especially if they're wild. Mix this with her 'no fear' attitude and danger soon follows.

Still, not all of her adventures here involve life or death danger. Many are stories that are just sweet, funny, creepy or enlightening. I frequently say that my wife is, "funner to watch than TV." Read on and see if you don't agree

- Steve

Chapter 1 - Meet the Wife

The attraction between a man and a woman is one of the least understood things in the human experience. It is particularly confusing for the man. Most guys know when they find a girl attractive, but it happens in so many ways. This girl might have nice hair, the next a bubbly personality. How can a guy figure out the attraction with so many variables?

The short answer is - he can't. He guesses, he changes his mind, he dumps and gets dumped. To be honest, it's a heart-breaking, demanding, and frustrating quest that just never seems to be met; and then, it is.

It happens differently for every person. Some experience love at first sight, some grow into a loving relationship. Others just develop a fascination over a period of time.

My love for my wife Shar did not occur overnight, but the fascination was always there. She is certainly pretty and I did notice that

What I *Didn't* Write

My wife Shar is *so* interesting that I didn't have room to write about these things:

- Washington baseball legend Frank Howard lived in her childhood home
- Famous actor Michael J. Fox introduced himself to Shar. She did not know who he was
- Shar asked for dirt for her birthday
- Her first boyfriend eventually became a mass murderer
- Shar dug up a wild turnip on a path near our house and served it up in our soup

right away, but what really set her apart was something in the way she moves. She's always moving and it has a certain bird-like characteristic. I was captivated.

She is small in stature and I've always weighed about twice her weight. She's so small that I joke that she comes in a 'convenient carry-around pack.' She's short (so that she can't see my bald spot) and a bit hard of hearing (so she can't hear my snoring). Now *that's* what I call a perfect match.

Travel Twofer

A vacation with Shar is always full of surprises. What would your spouse buy as a souvenir from Niagara Falls? At left we see that Shar purchased this nice, all-metal digging bar! She was thrilled to have such a useful, rock-busting souvenir of our trip. Try prying a root out with your Canada t-shirt.

At left we see Shar vacationing in downtown London. As the sun sets, we're torn as to which of the world-class tourist destination to see first. The London Eye? Big Ben? Buckingham Palace??? Shar chose to visit this Embankment Plane tree in a nearby park. Not too plain for us, though.

When I say Shar is fun to watch, consider these two examples from a softball game at her family reunion. First, Shar hit a ball and ran to first, losing her hat and both flip-flops on the way. Later, while she was playing in left field, I hit a monster drive that was likely 30 feet over her head and into a large tree. As the ball soared over her head, she jumped about 4" in the air to catch it. How cute is that?

Perhaps it's just me, but consider these things about Shar that I find entertaining, intriguing, or just plain interesting:

- Shar folds clothes in such a precise and repeatable manner that they stack perfectly. In fact, my closet always looks like a model home – unless I actually touch something. She 'rotates the stock' so that the newly folded clothes go on the bottom and all clothes wear out evenly. Who does that?!
- She always must touch any clothes she's interested in. If she doesn't like the feel, the purchase is off
- If there's no open seat in the room, she'll come sit on my lap
- To purify soil and kill any weed seeds, she once baked a large batch of dirt in the oven. I didn't ask what's for dinner *that* day
- Shar is a minimalist. When I met her she had 5 chairs, one table and 2 beds in a two bedroom apartment. That was pretty much all the contents. We collect nothing. A friend of my son Ross came over one day and told Ross upon leaving that our house was, "nice, but empty."

Mostly, I think I enjoy Shar's joyful exuberance. Whenever she sees me she smiles at me – which is pretty exceptional and the way a good wife shows she loves her husband. She is very serious about taking good care of me, and I let her.

Perhaps I am a bit jaded. She is my wife, after all. But I challenge you to read this book and see if you don't enjoy these stories about her as much as I enjoy telling them.

Message in a Bottle

Shar found this 1950's vintage milk bottle half buried in an embankment about 8 years ago. She pulled it out of the mud with the moss and fern intact. She then brought it to our kitchen where it has been carefully tended since. To her, the fern and moss are just as important as the bottle. She now has two ferns and a substantial amount of moss that are the off-spring of these original plants. She wants to develop either plants that grow naturally in a bottled environment or really tiny plants. Seriously. Wonders never cease!

Chapter 2 - Urban Wildlife

Neighborhood Chicken

Urban wildlife is just what you think it is. Most of us have periodic encounters with wildlife of some form or another. Few, however, actively seek these encounters. My wife, however, insists on sharing her love of animals with the tamed or wild animals that she meets - God help them.

As an example, her son Caleb's class raised chicks from eggs one year. When the experiment was over, Shar wanted to keep a chick. In fairness, she's always had a fascination with chickens. She'd raised chickens as a child and had many of them over the years before she met me. Having just married her, I couldn't deny her the pleasure of having another one, could I?

We lived in her house, a nice 4 bedroom model on a 1/4 acre lot in Northern Virginia at the time. The logistics of having a chicken were maybe not as well thought out as they could have been. Our unfinished basement seemed like a reasonable place to host a little chick. She and Caleb did seem to enjoy the little chick - what could go wrong?

Over the next few weeks and months, Caleb's interest wore off, but Shar continued to develop a relationship with that chick - who would follow her around like her mother as she worked in the garden or in various activities around the house. All in all, things seemed to be working out fine.

Unfortunately, little chickens do grow up to be big chickens. Six months later, there was a lot of soul searching as we started to hear the first crows of a young rooster.

Our neighbors did ask some tough questions. One day, one of our neighbors asked me why we were raising the chicken. "Do you plan to get some eggs," she asked in a most helpful way, trying to give me a way out. "No, it's a rooster," I said. "Oh ... so do you think you'll eat it when it gets grown?"

"No," I replied, "My wife is a vegetarian." That's usually how that kind of conversation ended.

To make matters worse, a grown rooster can get 'feisty'. The rooster decided that it needed to defend itself and our yard from everything else. It was getting harder to love this chicken as it started terrorizing every wild and domestic animal that approached our yard. To placate it, we did the only reasonable thing you can do in a cozy neighborhood with 1/4 acre lots and close neighbors. We got two hens.

Well, not really hens. More like 'teenage' hens. We were at a nearby fair where we bought 2 'pullets' - which is code for hens that are too young to lay eggs. Protecting these new hens did seem to at least help the rooster's attitude. It looked like we might be able to keep the entire new family together - until they all got lost one day.

Recipe for 'Vegetarian Chicken'

My brother's grandfather-in-law gave us this excellent recipe for 'Vegetarian Chicken':

Start with a board about 18" x 18" x 1" thick. Take a grown chicken (dead) and dip in boiling water to remove its feathers. Place the chicken on the board (you do not need to remove its organs for this recipe). Take some straw from the pen, and place it atop the chicken. Sprinkle with paprika, salt, and seasonings. Bake at 350° for 45 minutes. Remove the chicken from the oven and let cool for 5 minutes. Slide the chicken and the straw off the board and into the trash. Eat the board.

It turns out that chickens don't really have a very good sense of direction, or decorum, or pretty much any sense at all. When we realized they'd run away, there was a bit of panic, but we all thought they'd be back by nightfall, as usual. It was a little cold that night. Actually I think it was freezing when our neighbor came by. "Nice to see you," I said cheerfully. "Your chickens are under our deck," is all he could tell me, and then he turned and stormed back to the warmth of his house.

An hour later, our chickens were successfully coaxed back into our basement, and the 'jig was up'. The next weekend we built a pen for the chickens on some nearby land. Now the chickens were free to roam in a pen far from humans and neighbors. Unfortunately, there were foxes, raccoons, owls, weasels, and nosy neighborhood kids in the area, thus bringing this chapter to a rather swift close. At least we did get some eggs, so I guess the overall experience was a success.

Rabbit in the House

There's not a lot of things cuter than a baby rabbit. Shar and I heard the squeaking of this rabbit before we found it. It was alone in a bush near the front of our house. Shar looked around for the parents, but it seemed the little rabbit was an orphan.

Shar has a natural love of wildlife and there is nothing more attractive to her than a poor helpless creature, especially if it is very cute. We (the 'collective we') decided to adopt this poor, helpless animal and nurse it back to be returned to the wild - just like on the TV shows.

I'm pleased to say that we were very successful with that little rabbit. After a few hours, some water, and a special blend of 'rabbit favorites' that Shar blended up, the little guy started hopping like he was coming around nicely. We started him on lettuce and greens, and he quickly was hopping in his cardboard box with increasing vigor. The little guy was really cute, and the kids loved watching him.

One day, about two weeks later, we came downstairs to find that our little rabbit friend had escaped the confines of its cardboard box. We looked around, but really could not tell where he'd run off to. Shar put a plate of lettuce down in the kitchen, and a bowl of water in case the rabbit got thirsty.

Find what I touched in the Closet

Shar's a meticulous cleaner. I am not. Here we see what my closet, organized by Shar, usually looks like on any given day. Can you tell what items I've touched?

This one is easy because I'm the only one who can reach up to where the jeans are haphazardly 'folded'. I do that sometimes ... sorry dear ...

Having a rabbit loose in your house is not as stressful as you might think. At first, we would look for him by quickly opening doors and jumping into rooms 'SWAT team' style. No matter how hard we looked, though, we never saw the actual rabbit. We did however, see plenty of 'evidence' that the rabbit was alive and well, and soon after, apparently able to go up and down the stairs. He was really growing up - apparently. Weeks went by. Gradually our lives returned to normal, rabbit droppings aside.

Then, one day, our fateful reunion took place. Shar and I were downstairs when Caleb yelled, "I see the rabbit!" We jumped into action and tore up the steps eventually cornering the little guy in Caleb's room. When we closed the door, we finally could see that the end was near - one way or the other.

Caleb's room was not large, maybe 12 x 15 feet. The rabbit had really grown, and was probably 9" long. He was unbelievably fast. Trying to catch a little thing like this that is so delicate and so fast is really tricky. It was absolutely impossible to just grab it. We tried unsuccessfully for a while before deciding to force him into Caleb's little walk-in closet. When we closed the closet door and we were all inside with the rabbit, we determined we had won; it was just a matter of time.

Sometimes 'just a matter of time' can take a while. In that closet, perhaps 4' by 7', we all sat on the floor next to each other, legs extended. As we attempted to grab it, that little rabbit took off doing a 26 mile marathon, 7' at a time. We would reach for it and it would take off to the other side of the closet. The next person would reach for it and it would start back again. Each lap would involve going across all our legs with hands flailing, reaching, grasping, and invariably, missing. Eventually the poor little guy did tire out and we were able to touch him, but it probably took 5 minutes to actually grab him in a way where we could hold him and put him in a container.

With all of us sweating in that little closet, including the rabbit, we decided that he was ready to be returned to the wild. He may die of starvation, but *nothing* was going to catch him. We returned him to the same spot where we found him and he was gone almost instantly.

In the weeks and months after that, I would periodically see that rabbit while mowing the lawn or working in the yard. Shar also reported seeing the rabbit and as it grew up we'd see it periodically, more or less in the same group of bushes from where we first saw him. There are a lot of wild animal raising stories that I've heard, but this one really did have a happy ending, and I guarantee you - nothing ever caught *that* rabbit.

Ross's Duck

When he was growing up, Shar would periodically ask my son Ross what type of animal he'd want if he had his choice. He always had the same response, "I'd like a duck." Shar was determined to get him one, although we still lived in that 1/4 acre neighborhood. I'd say our neighbors were 'amused' by the variety of animal and wildlife experiences they'd experienced coming from our house, but I didn't really want to ask them. I preferred to think that her offer to get Ross a duck was one of those nice things you say to a kid to humor them; like an offer to give him a pony.

Then, of course, the day finally happened. She was absolutely beaming when she came in the house that day. Love is a funny thing. I love my wife so much that I looked right past the box and focused on her smile. She was so happy! There's not much a guy can do when the love of his life smiles at him like that, so I just smiled back.

Then she said, "I've got a duck for Ross!"

The box held a little bird, perhaps 3" tall, with some rags around it to keep it warm. It started to emit a sound. Not a 'cheep' like a chicken, but more of a distress call. While I watched, it started flopping around. It must have been pretty young. As I watched, it started flapping its wings a bit more vigorously and it started to get louder. Shar tried to calm it, but this bird was wild.

She took the bird downstairs to show Ross, who was playing on the computer. He took one look, and then decided that maybe a duck was not the right animal for him after all. By now, the 'duck' was starting to get increasingly agitated. Perhaps he sensed that Ross was not the ideal parent as well. Shar took the bird upstairs again and let it loose on the floor ("maybe it just needs to move around a bit"). In my mind, I could see that rabbit jumping all over our house again. What would this bird do - fly around?

Shar confessed that the bird was not actually a duck. In fact it was a goose - a Canadian goose. Apparently she was at Fair Oaks Mall and had seen this bird walking around by itself and her mothering instinct took over.

The bird did need to move around a bit. It needed to move around a lot more, at a high rate of speed. It also needed to yell a little more. The scene began to change perspective. It had quickly changed from Shar's 'mission of mercy' to what more closely resembled a kidnapping, or maybe a murder scene (as the bird was telling it). That goose was out to tell the world of this injustice to all birds. I had visions of the neighbors calling PETA, the SPCA, and the World Wildlife Foundation and having us arrested.

Shar used her cat-like quickness to grab the bird who was now screeching even louder than before. Mercifully, and without saying a word, she put the bird back into its cardboard box. I didn't even need to say anything. I let the bird do the talking.

Twenty minutes later she was back with a heartwarming tale of the bird's triumphant return to a group of geese that were swimming around the same lake. Ross, Shar and I have never, ever mentioned Ross's desire to have a duck again.

Crow Movie

To the casual reader it must seem that these stories have been carefully documented over a long period of time, but the truth is - this type of story happens so frequently, I can't even remember most of them. I can guarantee that for every story I remember, there's at least one that I've forgotten. I can honestly say that she really does want to help these creatures, but sometimes it doesn't work out exactly as she'd like.

Take yesterday. I was reviewing pictures and movies that I had recorded on my phone. One movie in particular caught my eye. I had forgotten it, and when I showed Shar, she said she'd forgotten it as well. But then she remembered.

As always, it started with a wildlife creature in need (cue dream sequence)...

There she was, walking down the sidewalk in our neighborhood, minding her own business. Then, in a nearby field she heard the 'Caw Caw' of a young crow. She looked around, but there were no parent crows nearby. On the spot, she decided that she would adopt this bird and that she would heal it. Who knows, maybe this bird would even make a great pet (think Uncle Billy's crow from 'It's a Wonderful Life'). Yes, she would be the envy of all her friends with this crow on her shoulder. Even if the bird didn't want to be a pet, she could release it into the wild after her gentle care. At least that's her recollection of the beginning of the story.

Cut now to the movie. The scene opens with the 'little' bird (who actually appears to be nearly full grown) in the side yard to our house. Shar has placed three objects in front of the bird in her hand. One is a small bowl of water ("it seemed dehydrated," she reminded me as we watched), as well as two plates of something that I can only assume is her best estimate of what a juvenile crow eats.

There is a horrible racket from the skies. The camera clearly records the sound of two adult crows with agitated 'CAW CAW' calls. On the ground, the injured 'teen' bird is placed next to the bowl of life saving water. Unfortunately, it is too stupid to drink the water. Instead, it 'caws' back to the other birds, and attempts to run into a nearby bush.

Now the hero returns, and she attempts to grab the 'teen' from the bush. Like many teens, the bird doesn't recognize that the adult is actually trying to save its life. Overhead, the adults scream with renewed vigor and circle close to our hero, who finally is able to grab the bird from the bush with her hand (better than two in the bush), and return it to the food and water.

The camera now pans to the nearby ground where two ominous shadows fly by, increasing in volume and now near our hero's head. Undaunted, she attempts to provide the water directly to the beak of the bird. Unfortunately, the young crow now joins the two other birds in the sky with a shrieking sound. Perhaps they are singing for joy over the actions of our hero in saving this young bird.

One thing is certain; the bird is not interested in the water. Shar puts the bird down, and gently pushes it over to the plate of food. Now a brief aerial attack begins and the star of our show retreats from the scene. She is smiling as she returns to the camera. Her mission is complete. She has reunited the young bird with its parents. The cameraman is laughing so hard that he can barely hold the camera straight.

After I'd seen that movie I remembered exactly how this ended. We went inside, leaving the birds to their reunion. When I went outside the next day, and for several days thereafter, those birds continued to 'CAW CAW' at me. I don't speak bird, but I'm pretty sure that what they were saying was, "Thanks for a job well done."

You're welcome crows.

Exciting Crow Rescue Movie Clips

Top Left: Shar provides food and drink for young crow needing rescue.

Top Right: Foolish crow runs into bushes, Shar rescues bird from bushes

Bottom Left: Thirsty crow gets 'watered'. Momma bird shadow at top right

Bottom Right: Shar observes mother crow. Child crow is now done being rescued. Mission Success!

The Bird Who Flew Without Wings - Twice!

So you now understand that Shar really does enjoy animals. There have been many animals in her life; some her pets, some just her acquaintances. We have all experienced the cruel nature of life. But sometimes the good guys win.

We had a bird at one point that had a nest in a nook in the back of our house. I'm not sure where the nook was, but Shar gave me a daily update on the status of that bird's nest. There was no special effort to take care of the mother bird, but just a curiosity that people have about a bird's nest that they see often.

One day I arrived home from work to find that we had a new houseguest. Apparently a neighborhood cat had attacked the nest, and Shar had found the mother dead outside the nest. Of the 3 babies, only a single one was left. Shar had found the baby calling out and decided to take it inside the house in case the cat returned.

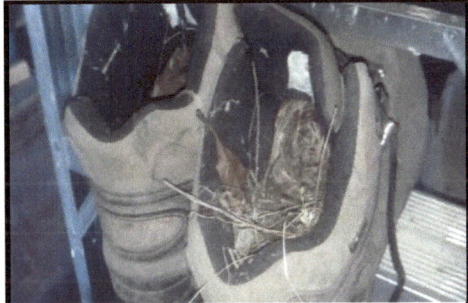

Our barn has its share of mice and vermin. We keep our boots on a ladder to prevent mice from entering. We recently found that a bird had built this nest in my boot! We watched intently as the wren raised its family safe from predators and the elements inside our barn. Not sure I'll ever wear those boots again, though.

There are some situations that even I, a full-grown man, find difficult to tolerate. One is the senseless killing of cute little baby birds by neighborhood cats. The other is the adoption of said baby birds by a grown woman that lives in my house.

I shouldn't say that I didn't *like* this little bird. How can you not like a cute little baby bird? What kind of monster doesn't like cute little baby birds? Apparently the kind of monster that doesn't like baby birds is the kind that hears the baby bird in the middle of the night 'cheeping' to be fed. Actually ... this little bird kind of grew on me.

17

Shar brewed up a special solution of worms, eggs, and some secret ingredients that seemed to change day by day. Shar fed the little bird with a human baby medicine syringe, slowly releasing an ounce or two per feeding. Apparently the little bird and Shar finally settled on a recipe that the bird liked and the adoption became official.

As you might have noticed, I'm accustomed to having wild animals of all varieties in the house with us. Day by day I'd come home to find the little bird gradually growing in size and activity. It was still pretty helpless, but it was starting to grow feathers.

We had a call during this time that Shar's brother was ill and was being treated at Mayo clinic in Minnesota. His wife wanted company and asked Shar if she could join her and Shar accepted. Fearing that *I* would be called in to service with the bird, I asked her what the plans were for the bird. "I'll take it with me," was all she said. The next day, Shar took the bird, put it in a loose fitting pocket of a sun dress, and went through the X-ray machine and onto the plane. A few hours later she drove to her hotel and fed the bird, no fuss, no muss.

She stayed with her brother and sister-in-law in Minnesota while he healed, and then repeated the entire exercise on the way back. She was beaming when she returned. "The bird never 'cheeped' on the plane," she said. I guess that's what proud parents of birds say when their kids have no problem flying. She'd flown over 1000 miles in each direction with that bird never leaving her pocket.

The bird continued to grow and developed a handsome set of feathers. It now flitted about on tables, counters, stairs or floors practicing with its new wings. I remained impervious, reading my paper as it ate some seed from a paper plate or crashed into a wall while trying to make a tricky turning maneuver. Periodically I'd take a napkin and clean some 'reminders' from the floor or a chair. This bird had really grown, and then … it was gone.

One day Shar took the bird outside while she did some yard work. While she and I both watched, the bird spread its wings and flew to a nearby tree. Shar ran over to the tree to recover the bird, but it simply flew to a higher branch - and out of her reach (teenagers!). She called me over and asked me to reach it but it was too high. Shar became increasingly concerned that the bird would not fly back to her, and it never did. The bird had officially grown into an adult. For many days Shar would leave out some seed, and she did *see* the bird again, but there were no long gazes, wing flips, or any sign that the bird was her dear, sweet baby. She really did miss that bird.

I'm not sure what ever happened to that bird, but imagine the stories it could tell about flying at 600 miles per hour at 35,000 feet.

Eggs

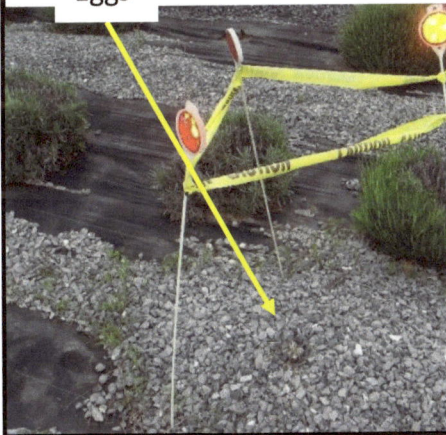

I was pleasantly surprised to find these pictures while looking for others for the book. The top picture shows four birds eggs that Shar found oddly enough in a row of bush plantings. At bottom, Shar's reaction to the finding and the protective shield that she established. The 'caution' tape sends a clear message to all predators to, "stay away!" You're probably thinking what kind of person erects police tape and protective markers for bird's eggs laid by a mother too lazy to put them in a nest?!? Shar does. My wife is worshiped and admired by stupid birds everywhere.

The Homing Parakeet

It's been a little over a month since I wrote about what Shar has done – but her exploits just keep on giving! The summer months are particularly productive because she has the opportunity to be out and about and is bustling with activity. This story started in an odd way with a gift from her brother, Doug.

Doug has always loved birds and knows how to handle them. Therefore, when he saw a parakeet in the parking lot of our local grocery store, he knew how to catch it. Before the day was over, Doug had put the bird in a nice cage and brought it to our house as a gift for Shar (or at least that's how their story goes).

The bird, a pretty blue parakeet, has taken residence in our kitchen. Doug was kind enough to clip the bird's wings a bit, but not so much that the bird couldn't fly at all. We decided to call the bird Popeye as he has a bit of an attitude, doesn't like to be touched, and struts around like he owns the place. Shar couldn't have been more enchanted.

Funny, I don't remember being asked if we could keep the bird.

In the middle of the summer, we frequently keep the door open on our back deck to get fresh air. Shar insists that the screen 'stops the breeze', so the door is frequently wide open, and, well … old habits die hard. We hadn't had the bird two days when Popeye flew out the sliding glass door and was gone.

This might surprise some people. Some people keep their birds *in* the cage. Shar likes more of a 'free range' type of arrangement, with the door open to allow the bird to 'stretch its wings'. Unfortunately, stretching sometimes leads to flapping, and flapping sometimes leads to … well, birds out the back door.

The situation was not helped when Shar's mother called within an hour of when the bird went missing. Shar couldn't bring herself to tell her mother what had happened to Doug's gift, so she fibbed and said the bird was fine.

Things were not getting better. She was distraught all night.

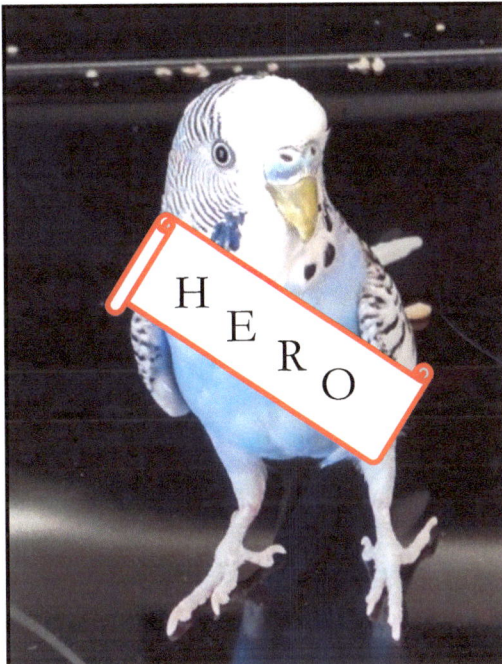

Popeye the Bird – American Hero

Shortly after I wrote this story, I needed to add this update. A book I recently read about 'Dog Heroes' had a story about a dog who filled his owner's back yard with poo. A subsequent thief was captured because of the dog's poo on his shoe, *linking him to the scene of the crime!* Some hero ...

By that standard consider this amazing act of bird bravery. While eating seeds nearby one day, Popeye observed a flame caused by a misplaced paper plate on our stove top. Shar, working on the other side of the room, was distracted. Popeye let out a piercing squawk, which alerted Shar who quickly put out the fire. As a result, no lives were lost. Popeye's quick action is hereby recognized. Had Shar not rallied quickly, I may be telling the story about how Popeye, a small bird, actually put that fire out. **Hurrah brave Popeye!**

When I came home the next day, I was pleasantly surprised to see Popeye in the large oak tree in front of our house. He was about 40' up, looking down with a rather superior air. Shar was there, of course, pointing out the bird, and making sure the cage was available if Popeye had a change of heart. She put new food in the cage, cleaned it out nicely, opened the door, and even put a little ladder up into the cage. Popeye would have nothing to do with it.

The next day I came home late, and Shar told me that she'd seen Popeye again. This time it was in a birch tree near our house. When she saw him, she'd quickly moved the cage down to the base of the tree and monitored the situation. She was elated that the ruse had worked, somewhat, and that she'd seen that Popeye had eaten some of the seed. All was not lost.

That night there was a terrible storm. A cold rain fell hard most of the night, and lightning woke us several times.

I went to work the next morning, and Shar put the cage out next to the birch tree again. When she checked later Popeye was back in the cage, and he wasn't coming out. He'd had enough. I joked with Shar that with the intensity of that storm I was surprised there weren't more birds crammed into that cage.

So now he's back to ruling our kitchen. He sits on top of his cage most days, occasionally flying over to the sliding glass door to speak to some birds in the woods nearby. He flies, but not particularly well. He likes to buzz around my head when he flies. I think it's because I'm usually the tallest object in the room, but it might just be to remind me of who is boss.

Shar jokes that she'll make him a 'homing parakeet', free to fly out any time and then return when things get rough in the woods. At least I hope she's joking. The last thing we need is a feral parakeet in this neighborhood. Perhaps the hawks would disagree.

Chapter 3 - Home Life

Making Things a Litter bit Better

Can a day go by without a story for this book? I was driving home from work one day, talking with my brother on the phone (hands-free, please!) when I saw a very unusual sign. 'How could a sign like that exist?' I thought, and then … well I'm getting ahead of myself.

Shar has always been super conscientious of trash in our neighborhood. As long as I've known her she's spent perhaps 10 days a year cleaning trash from our roadways, nearby woods, or any natural spot within walking distance. She has a great love of nature and a deep respect for its preservation. Several times a year I find bags and bags of trash piled up for disposal – the result of her personal crusade to keep our neighborhood clean.

I have spent time cleaning a community park, or a nearby road for various charitable reasons. I think that is a civic duty for everyone. But then, I only clean up once or twice a year. I can't even imagine spending so much time cleaning community property. But I am not my wife.

I've had several occasions where I return home to see her with a trash bag in hand, waving and smiling at me, embedded in a deep bush filled with discarded paper. I completely support her in this, as do my neighbors, and the people that drive by our neighborhood. But really - does she have to clean up so often? The answer is yes; yes she must.

San Tomas Aquino Watershed Cleanup

A friend from work in California, Matt, was leading this cleanup. When I told Shar, she *demanded* that I buy her a plane ticket so that she could help. What kind of person flies 3000 miles to pull paper cups, tennis balls and tires out of creek weeds? My wife! When it was over after 2 hours she requested that she be allowed to continue. Matt really didn't know what to say.

So I was not surprised when I saw the sign, but wait … I'm still getting ahead of myself.

Not everyone in our community appreciates such a timely response to the blight caused by sign encroachment into our neighborhoods. Politicians, karate studios, sofa salespeople, and others regularly place 'temporary' signs up advertising their candidates or their wares. I would say that Shar is 'largely intolerant' of such signs. In fact, when she sees one in our community, she will stop her truck, pick up the sign, and put it in the bed for disposal. While this might not be a 'good neighbor' policy, it does promote a clean community, and I have not heard of a neighbor complaint – or so I thought, until this day.

My brother Bruce knows Shar well. Often Shar will get a bag and start cleaning trash at a family gathering (hers or mine). So Bruce was not surprised when I told him what this sign said. As I was nearing my house, I saw Shar – smiling and waving – her natural pose when she sees me come home. "Come with me," was all I could say. And we walked to this offensive sign.

I could barely contain myself as I chatted with Bruce and led Shar to the sign – which was literally right in front of our house. She stood by the sign so that I could take a picture and send it to Bruce. He was surprised and shared a laugh when we saw the sign – which I still thought was a direct attack on Shar's neighborhood cleanup efforts.

I asked Shar about what she thought about the sign. Here I would gather some insight into the events that led to this atrocity. "You mean the school sign?" she said. "Well yes, the school sign, but more importantly, the sign *underneath* it – what did you think about *that*?" I asked.

"I didn't see that sign," she said. So, it was done. Here's the sign:

"Bruce," I said, "I think someone who had a sign torn down must finally be seeking revenge!" While he listened, I discovered who perpetrated this crime – the Fairfax County Police!

Maybe I'm a bit old fashioned, but I prefer to litter without formal direction.

When I finally told Shar this story, she surprised me a bit. I showed her this picture of the sign and she told me the rest of the story:

"I asked the county to come out and clean up the roads," she said. Apparently the county has some learning to do about litter cleanup.

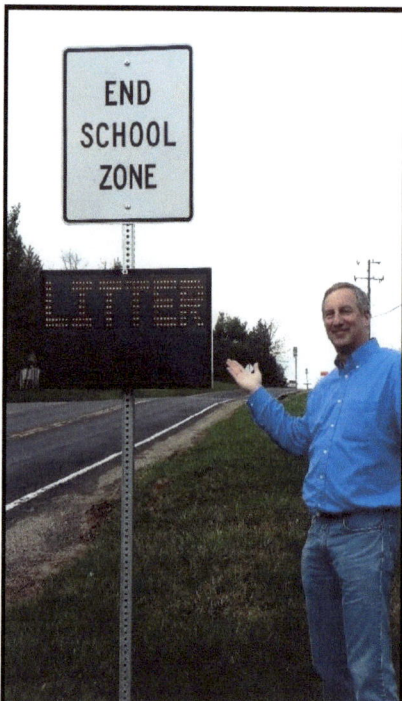

Litter, Please

Native Americans shed a tear as a result of this message. What terrorist organization can support littering so overtly you ask? The Fairfax County Police! A mile away, a larger sign says, "Litter Cleanup – please drive safely." Missing from this simple picture are the pulsing red and blue lights that suggest – Litter Here! I considered dumping my trash on the ground to support local law enforcement.

Dirty Work

Perhaps you've been part of someone else's 'Master Plan' at some point in your past. This, of course, requires a 'Master'. I think you can probably guess who that Master will be in this story.

It all started rather simply. My wife was doing some perusing on the internet and found a reference to a free publication on erosion protection. There was a catch, however. The publication was created by a county government office in California, and was only available to residents of that county. We live in Virginia. Apparently erosion protection documents are very difficult to find in our home state.

Most people would acknowledge that they don't live in that county and move on. Certainly this information was available somewhere on the internet. Perhaps there was a search page that provided different free documentation, or perhaps free publications in one's own county. Most people would continue their search elsewhere - perhaps a visit to the library, or a discussion with a local erosion specialist.

But this web page promised something that was not available anywhere else. This pamphlet, which teased with a cover and a few nice graphics of its inside contents, was 'special'. The cover photo in particular looked very much like the *exact* erosion problem we were facing. The inside photos looked glossy, and it looked like it was chock full of really good erosion protection information. I had to agree, this did look like *the* erosion booklet for us. Efforts to 'enlarge' the picture of the cover didn't help, and Shar's desire to have this 32-page, 4-color glossy book was peaked.

In the middle of this all I could think was, 'couldn't they just put this out as a web page, or maybe a PDF?' But this was back before people made sense of the internet or shared their hard earned county information. Things were about to take a bad turn.

Shar looked at me and said, "We've got to get this book." I smirked but was met with a hard look. She followed with an expression that I'd seen before many times. She was staring off in to the distance - not unlike the great schemers of our time. Unfortunately, this look usually included a partner in crime, and I was the only one available.

"My sister lives in California!" she said. "We can pretend that we live there!" she exclaimed. Now the plan was coming together. I shook my head in agreement. She could pose as her sister Linda, have it mailed to Linda's address in California. Linda would then forward it to us - a perfect plan!

There was only one snag. Apparently, she had more information. "I'm afraid I can't call," she said. "I called the lady earlier today and she said that she can't send it to me in Virginia because we don't live in the county." Hmmm...

"I'm sure she'd recognize my voice, so I can't call back again." All I could muster was a grunt. I couldn't even shake my head in agreement. You didn't need to be a genius to see where this was going. "You could pose as Rob, though," she said, with a smile that was classic Shar.

I was trapped.

"We've got to call soon," she continued, "their office is closing soon." I returned a stare that defined my position on this. I would help, but begrudgingly. "Get me my address," I said, preparing for the part I was destined to play. I'd done some acting in high school.

To be honest, I didn't know much about my brother-in-law Rob. He was a doctor, which was intimidating enough. Shar brought his address and I read it over several times. Time was working against us, and I needed some answers. The preparation continued,

"What are his kid's names again?"

"You don't need his kid's names, you're talking to a county agent about an erosion pamphlet," she reminded me.

No matter I thought, their names are Alex and Kaylan. I was ready for this. But wait, was it Kayla? Darn, I remembered now that she preferred to go by Genevieve. Why was this so hard?!

Shar dialed the number and I tried to breathe easy. This was in a simpler time, when the county agent didn't have caller ID (or did they?). How hard could it be? The conversation went something like this:

"County Extension Office, this is Marla, how can I help you?"

"Yes, this is Rob Wood, from California, I'd like to request that you send me your pamphlet on erosion protection."

Upper Salinas-Las Tablas Resource Conservation District

and the

San Luis Obispo County
Planning and Building Department

Cover Up Story

EROSION CONTROL HANDBOOK

A Practical Guide to Erosion Control and Sediment Reduction

Third Edition
July 2005

RCD
Conserving Resources
Providing Service Since 1951

The Holy Grail of Erosion Control

This Erosion Control handbook that was so elusive in 2003 that it forced me to commit petty fraud. Now available on the internet, the real 'Cover Up Story' in its title is why they couldn't put this on-line in 2003 when we needed it.

Nailed it! It was just a matter of time before 32-pages of glory were coming my way. But wait, why did I say 'from California'? Who does that other than people trying to scam true Californians? I remained cool.

"Ok Rob," already I sensed some trepidation on her part - perhaps my act was *too* good.

"Can you give me your address?"

Like Rob himself I read the address, my confidence growing as I concluded with,

"... Santa Maria, California 93455."

"Can you tell me what county that's in Rob?"

????

Um ... that's in ... Santa Maria County,"

I said, my edge substantially dulled. I hoped that there was such a thing as Santa Maria County (post fact-check information — no, there is no such thing as Santa Maria County in California)

"Well Rob, she continued, this pamphlet is only available to residents of San Luis Obispo County." And it was done.

"Can you sell me a copy?"

"I'm sorry Rob, but we have very limited production and only a few copies left" ...

There was a long pause. I considered my options. I could ask 'pretty please', but this lady was a hard bargainer. I considered bribing her, but she'd already said that money was not an issue for her. I looked at Shar who had the panicked look of someone who was not going to learn about erosion protection. I said the only thing I could say,

"Oh ... well, OK then. Thanks," and I hung up.

Way to rise to the occasion Steve.

The disappointment was palpable.

There was a brief silence, and then Shar said, "I guess I can't trust you to do my dirty work," and walked away. Which of course, left me to think, 'what dirty work?'

My Nice Brother

I'm pretty blessed to come from a family with lots of nice people. I had always thought that I was a product of that circumstance, but I found out differently one day a few years ago.

Shar was talking with my brother on the phone that day, and I could tell they were having quite an animated conversation. She was laughing and cheery and seemed disappointed when he had to leave the conversation. She hung up and announced to me, "Your brother Mark is so nice!"

Many people would have left that statement hanging there, boosting their husband's pride through association. Not my wife, though.

She continued, "He's sooo nice. You know, I think he's the nicest one in your family." And *that's* where she left it.

I waited patiently for her to say, 'aside from you, of course', and waited. There was a palpable quiet in the room. Even the crickets took a break to see what was going to happen.

I thought for a moment then realized that perhaps she was not aware of her omission, and made an overture with my hand and arms rolling as if to say, 'and ...'.

Silence.

Finally, she piped up, "Oh wait!" she said, "You know, your Dad is very nice too."

More silence.

I realized she was probably putting me on, but when I looked at her, she had no expression of humor. In fact, she had the expression of someone with great conviction like someone describing Hitler as a 'bad man'. She turned as if to leave, and I followed for a bit, waiting for that funny little laugh of hers and a, 'Ha! Ha! Had you going there.' Apparently the only place she had me going was behind her.

After a bit, I veered off, uncertain of my position with this woman. I was a bit upset, and decided to 'fight' my rival head on! – In the nicest way possible, of course.

I dialed my brother. He answered, chipper and happy to talk with me. I wasn't fooled. I suspected he was in on the joke as well. I described what Shar had said and he replied with this classic response:

"That's funny you should mention that, Steve. Beth (his wife) and I were just talking about you, and she said how nice *you* were. She said that she so enjoys it when you come over and how your jokes are so funny, and how you're so good with the kids … ," etc. It continued for some time, but then *he* got in the act and started to compliment me as well. My head was swelling with pride. Yes, at least my brother Mark understood how good, how nice, how noble I was.

But wait! I'd fallen for his trick!

Then I realized the truth. My brother Mark *is* nicer than me.

There was no denying it. I was upset for a few hours, then I realized that there was only one thing that could make me feel better about this situation. Even today, whenever Shar asks me to do something that I really don't want to do, I can always turn to her, say no, and then add the clincher, "Well if you wanted that, you should have married the nice brother!"

What goes in a Bathtub (Part 1)

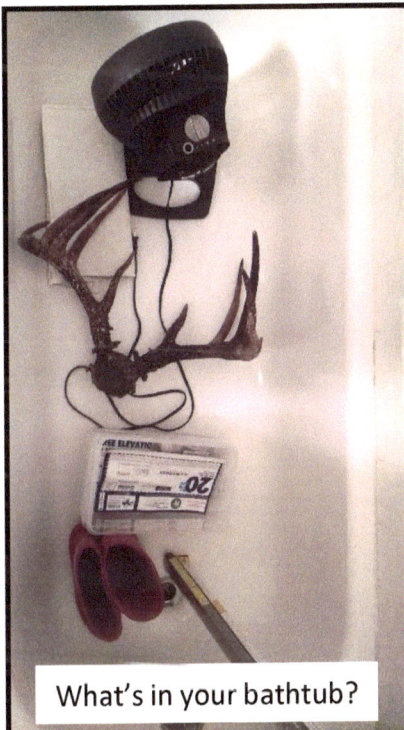

What's in your bathtub?

I don't believe that I've taken a bath in a tub at my own house since the 1980's. To be honest, I really prefer the shower. As a result, the bathtub in our house is frequently used for short-term storage of things destined for the attic or a new place in the house. I've taken some pictures of what's found its way to our tub at various times over the years. I'm always surprised when I look at these pictures at the diversity of stuff we find in our tub. Here's a good sampling:

- The deer antlers are some of the largest I've ever seen. Shar found them in the creek behind our house, cleaned them up, and they're under our glass table in the living room now.
- Coupons, coupons and more coupons – where are we supposed to keep all these things?
- The fan, rain boots and landscape fabric tell me its spring and time for gardening

Chapter 4 - Life in the Wild

As the title suggests, this chapter details life with my wild wife. I say wild, but she is actually very tame, a little shy, and very loving. A man can have a girlfriend, but a wife who sincerely loves and respects her husband is a treasure indeed. Throw in a little entertainment and a man may never leave the house.

Ah yes, entertainment. Imagination can be a wonderful thing. Just as kids play with toys, making cardboard boxes into spaceships, Shar has an active imagination with the things around her. Sure there's a wild side to her, but I find the imagination side just as interesting. This chapter captures some classic stories of Shar's adventures, at least as I remember them.

Take for instance this story from long ago.

'Miniature Cows'

If there's anything that Shar wanted after we bought some property (see the next chapter), it was to stock that property with animals. There was some hesitation, however, regarding what type of animals. The property was well suited to cows or sheep and had fields of hay that would be excellent for their feed.

Although she wanted cows, she was very concerned about how she would maneuver such big animals with such a small frame herself. There was also concern that a cow would step on her little foot - possibly causing serious injury. We ruled out sheep and goats as we'd require a colony of those to fill the property and the barn that we had would likely not hold that many of these animals.

She was delighted to find out one day that there was such a thing as a 'miniature' cow. Now lest you think that I'm joking, the internet can show you exactly the details of this contrivance. Living in the days before ubiquitous internet, she found a flyer about a show on 'Exotic Farm Animals' in nearby Kentucky and we were off the next weekend to see just how 'miniature' these cows actually were.

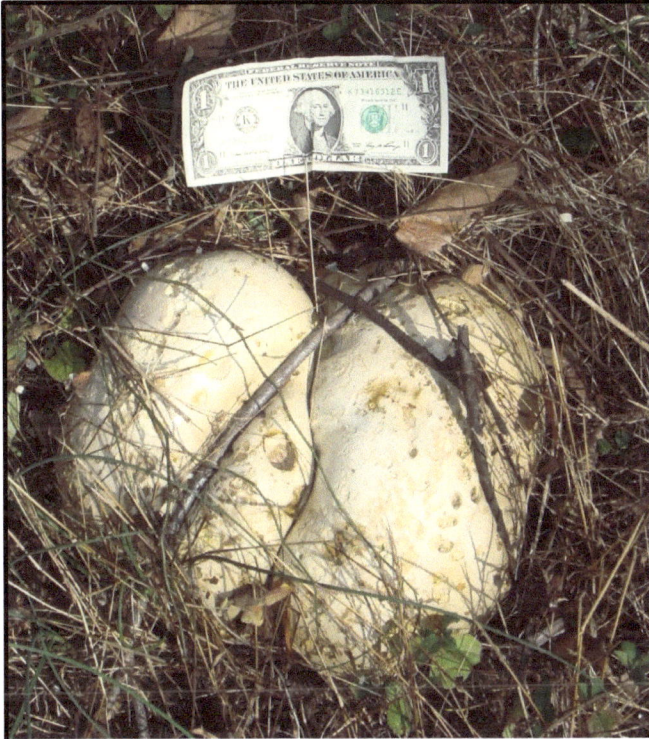

When you live with Shar you're going to end up with some pictures you can't explain. I don't even know what to say about this one ...

On the long car ride to Kentucky I thought about what we were doing. Just exactly what was the purpose of the miniature cow anyway? Would we milk them? Turn them into miniature hamburgers? Keep them as pets like that rooster in the previous chapter? My 'money pit' sensors suddenly went on high alert. I envisioned myself with $20,000 of miniature cows requiring feed, vets, fencing, etc. What would I tell the neighbors now if they asked what we were doing out there?

The state of Kentucky might as well have been a different planet. This fair had every kind of contrived animal you could conceive of in every shape, color and size. I must have heard 100 people telling me the benefits of alpaca wool, bizarre types of goat hair, or ostrich eggs. All I could think was that I was so grateful that I didn't already own a field full of alpacas, bizarre goats, or ostriches. That's all I needed was to be trying to sell some of this stuff.

And then, there it was. A little black calf, probably 200 pounds and 3 feet tall at the back. I was immediately drawn to it. It actually *was* cute, and I momentarily forgot that it was likely an economic disaster on hooves. Still, its little black eyes were friendly, and he seemed well-proportioned if not a bit thin. 'We can fatten him up', I thought - completely losing all grip on reality now that I'd seen this little thing.

Against all reason, I actually wondered, 'how much does this little guy cost?' Shar was completely consumed by the calf and would have changed its diapers if anyone had bothered to put some on it. She was sold, sold, sold, and I felt that the balance of financial power was swinging a little too closely to the bankruptcy side.

A helpful man emerged, beaming at the possibility of a new sale. Silently I wondered how many alpacas, bizarre goats, and ostriches he also owned. "She's a beauty," he offered. "Oh yes, she's *won-der-ful*," the wife said, with the italics thrown in. Now my resolve was up. Cute or not cute I would not be investing in anything as foolish as a cow that could at best provide only 400 quarter pounders. Then, a miracle occurred.

"I'd love to sell her to you," the man said. Shar's eyes widened as if to say 'sold!', "but I can't," he continued. "Her Momma would be very upset if I did." Now the plot thickened. "If you come over here," he said, "I'll show you her Daddy and he *is* for sale." I grabbed my wallet for protection.

We wandered over to an adjacent booth and looked inside. I was not prepared for what I saw. There, in a little paddock, was a not-so miniature bull. It probably weighed 600 pounds and was 4' high. In fairness, it *was* smaller than a regular cow, but it was definitely not *cute*. In fact, it looked a bit ornery and at 600 pounds, Shar recoiled at the thought of owning such a thing. I felt the warmth of my wallet remaining in my pocket.

We didn't buy a miniature cow that day, although I hear that they are now 'all the rage' (for cute farmers). Shar and I started the long drive home, she disillusioned, and me with a quiet smile on my face.

What goes in a Bathtub? (Part 2)

Here's a brief list of things that we've had in our bathtub or shower:

- Varmints – including rabbits, birds, snakes, turtles, chickens, dogs, frogs, and a variety of small animals (we had a lizard in our bathtub one time, very briefly)
- Refrigerators (although, in fairness, I put that in there)
- Chainsaws (where else would you put them?)
- Gasoline and lubricants
- Fans, books, paint cans, paint supplies
- Weed whackers
- Clothes/shoes
- Canned goods
- Tools

Snow shovels go in the shower, which actually makes sense, kinda

What does not go in a Bathtub?

- People (not in our bathtub anyway)

An Island Paradise

The internet is wonderful source of new information and ideas. Most of us get our 'new information and ideas' in the form of practical ideas for everyday problems. We own some property near our house that has a pond on it. It is a beautiful pond, and it seems to grow two things: 1.) algae in the summer (that's unfortunate), and 2.) ideas for my lovely wife.

Recently Shar uncovered an interesting story on the internet. While researching gardening ideas, she saw the story of a man in the Philippines (or some island nation) who built a floating island. The island was constructed with a net that holds thousands of plastic bottles to allow it to float. The man had then heaped a lot of dirt on top of the bottles to create a man-made island.

The beauty of this concept was that the island, which was tethered to his nearby houseboat, produced vegetation. The leafy vegetables planted on the island were watered by their roots, which sank down through the dirt and into the water below. Ingenious!

Of course, one great thing about the internet is that it shows the concepts that worked – if even for a short period. Never mind that we live in an area which receives plenty of natural rain for plants, the idea was hatched – we were going to build a floating island!

The first step in the building process was the gathering of hundreds or even thousands of empty plastic bottles. Everywhere we went we gathered bottles. Actually she gathered most of them because I had a morbid fear that the floating island project would result in a project of epic proportions for me – involving the collection of hundreds or thousands of empty plastic bottles along the shore of the pond. But Shar would not give up.

We bought drinks from every store, outlet, school or public place in the state. I had never particularly noticed her concern for my thirst until now. We rarely passed an opportunity to purchase hydration, using an unusual method; we bought drinks based not on flavor, but on the relative strength of their plastic bottle. Several times Shar even upgraded our drink from water to a different beverage – particularly if the original water bottle looked flimsy.

This pattern went on for weeks, and the pile of bottles gathering was becoming alarming to me. 'She might actually do this', I found myself thinking. I was terrified. Much as I thought the idea was pretty neat, I was scared that the execution might not be as good as reported on the internet. 'What's the worst that could happen?' I thought. Then I thought again about gathering thousands of bottles from the edges of the pond.

The concern escalated until one day in a nearby hardware store. As we neared the checkout counter, I saw her swerve to the nearby mini-fridge to pick two bottled waters. At this point, her thinking was that if there were only cans in the fridge, then I was probably not thirsty.

We put the waters in with our other purchases, and as soon as we'd paid for them she opened hers. She drank a bit while I finished checking out, and then she realized something awful about this bottle of water.

With a sneer on her face, she spoke in a too-loud voice saying, "These bottles are made out of plants!" The checkout guy looked at her with a confused look. "Look," she said, pointing at the label. Her face had the sickened look she usually reserves for particularly disgusting insects.

Clearly, she realized that a plant-based bottle would not do for her island project. Furthermore, we'd probably paid *extra* to get this bottle.

The clerk blinked, looked at her, and blinked again. There was no point in trying to explain. I paid quickly so that we could leave without going back to the returns department.

In the end, my fears were not realized. The giant pile of bottles did gradually dissipate into several full recycling bins over many weeks. I still wonder though what that checkout guy must think about how we treat the environment.

Pond Living

Having a pond on your property is wonderful feature. Most of the time, the pond takes care of itself, and there's nothing more relaxing than a little fishing or a boat ride. This little mini-chapter is dedicated to some of Shar's other ideas for how we should use the pond. In fairness to her, many of these ideas were suggested by others – some with viable business ideas, some with best intentions, and some with outright crazy ideas. Here's a quick summary of some of the ideas and issues associated with pond living:

We hadn't owned our property for more than a few days when we went for a visit. Our intent was to build a house and farm this land, living happily ever after. During the inspection, Shar noted that we'd need a place to live while we built the house. Spying the pond, she suggested that maybe a houseboat was the answer! It turns out – she'd always wanted a houseboat. I really didn't know what to say to that one. The pond is only a few acres in size, and a boat would have to pretty much just sit there. In the end, I think I convinced her that a trailer would be better, if only because trailers don't sink with all your possessions. Sorry about that one dear …

One problem with any pond is that when it rains very hard, you start to think about what might happen if the pond's dam, 'washed out.' It's funny how you'll never even consider that possibility when you buy a pond, but when it rains really hard for a few days and you watch the pond fill up completely, you can't help but think about what is downstream, and how expensive or deadly a burst dam might become. As luck would have it, we had 'help' with our pond shortly after we bought it. Shar invited a good-hearted engineer from the county to come out and take a look. He pointed out how the water from the pond should be coming out only from the one drain pipe, and not through a series of streams at the base of our pond wall. That was a very sad day.

Six months later, the pond was almost completely drained. Heavy equipment laid all over the property like toys in a sandbox and we realized that we could now be proud of our pond and its future safety record. The good news is that there was not enough water in it to support the boat that we could no longer afford. One sad note – I was able to watch beautiful Herons, Egrets, and other birds eat fish camped on the shores of our draining pond, picking out fish that I would never catch.

The Dam Project

Here heavy equipment is used to destroy fishing in our pond in the interest of 'safety'. Shar took the picture of this backhoe from the top of a giant pile of dirt removed from the primary retaining wall in the dam. She loves to stand on absurdly high and dangerous precipices.

Speaking of birds, there is nothing as majestic as the flight of the Canadian goose — especially if it's leaving your pond. These things can destroy your pond and grass, and no one likes to step in their 'leavings'. We make it a yearly ritual to cull (destroy) the goose eggs we find, but there still seems to be no shortage of geese. To make matters worse, there's a small island in the pond that acts as a hideout. It's no wonder those darned birds wear a black mask.

One of Shar's friends was excited to sell us on the idea of putting a fish farm on the property. He outlined in detail all the benefits and expected financial gains associated with turning our pond into a fish breeding business. His story had enough truth in it that even I considered it for a bit, but then I had to reconsider. Some of the fish we were going to be growing in our farm pond were actually salt-water fish. Now that *would* be a money maker if we could do that!

Shar's Bull

There are few things Shar enjoys more than re-telling the story of her capture of a massive bull. At the time, she was living with her parents on a farm in Florida. As she tells it, she was brushing her teeth when she saw out the window a massive red-colored bull running down the dirt road in front of her house.

Like most women, she ran down to see if she could catch it (OK, I know that's not like most women). Fortunately, she had a secret weapon. When she got down to the street, she opened a gate that faced the road, and the bull ran right into their fenced pasture. Normally, you might fear that the bull would gore a crazy 99 pound woman running around, but this bull was more interested in the cows that were grazing in that field.

After things calmed down a bit (we'll leave it at that), the family asked around where the bull came from. No one claimed the bull, and the family kept it for a while. When the time finally came to sell the bull, it was enormous. Shar recalls that when the bull was entered into the auction ring there was a notable crescendo of voices and whistles. It was the largest bull at the auction. Not many people would see a bull running down the street as a business opportunity, but as you know by now, not many people are like my wife.

Another Fish Story

No story about a fish farm would be complete without a description of a related pond owned by my in-laws. As the picture shows, it's a great place to relax. The shore on the right is where I first fished in this pond and, well ... let me go back.

When they purchased their pond, my mother-in-law stocked it with fish. As part of the stocking process she had to feed the fish every day for a while until they were acclimated.

I was excited to fish this new pond when we went for a visit. I really wasn't ready for what I experienced next, however. When I went down to the side of the pond, fishing rod in hand, all the fish came swimming up to me to get fed.

There's probably a fishing lesson in there somewhere, but I don't know where it is ...

Farm Science Review

Marriage involves many compromises, surprises, and last minute decisions. Here's a summary of a trip that Shar and I just returned from. I think many readers, especially those who are married, will relate to this one.

I was not too surprised when Shar expressed her desire to go to a Farm Science Review 500 miles from our house. As 'farmers' we (mostly she) likes to keep up with all the latest advances in farm technology. I initially told her to go ahead and go by herself, but then marriage stepped in – which is how I ended up in Ohio at the Farm Science Review.

On the drive up I was informed that I would not be attending the NFL's Football Hall of Fame while she would go to the review. Rather, we would go as a couple to the Farm Science Review, and then we would go as a couple to the Hall of Fame – except that she would not be setting foot in the Hall of Fame. And so with the itinerary set, we were on the road.

Traveling with my wife is one of the great joys of vacation life. She does not nag about my driving, and reads aloud books and keeps the conversation lively as we go down the road. The miles flew by and we were in Springfield Ohio before we knew it.

As I may have mentioned, I am not a farmer. I really did not know what to expect at the Review. Would I be chastised for my lack of farm savvy? I imagined boring lectures by experts in farm seed science or insect control. I was really not prepared for what I would see there.

On the drive over, I contemplated my situation. Could I hold my own with farmers from across the United States? Would I be singled out as an outsider? Fortunately, I had the ruddy tan of a 3 day golf getaway and jeans with a tee-shirt, which was as farm-like as I could get.

The Farm Science Review is not what you (or at least I) would expect. The whole atmosphere was like a giant American 'fair', but without the rides. The grounds were filled with about 20,000 people when we arrived, and I could not believe the size of the fairgrounds. As we arrived, yellow-vested parkers directed us to a parking spot that was probably a half-mile from the entrance to the event.

I was worried. My t-shirt was not warm enough. I scrambled frantically through my suitcase, looking for something in a 'camo' motif. In the end, I wore a golf pullover in to the Farm Science Review. The only good news was that no one would recognize me with my head down in shame all the time.

Shar was in her element. She jumped from exhibit to exhibit – asking questions, talking to vendors, asking questions about poultry netting, natural pesticides, native plantings, and of course – the highlight of the Farm Science Review – the Ohio State University Pawpaw grove.

I carried the bag with our stuff.

Don't get me wrong, I enjoyed the trip. I could not believe what I was seeing. I was starting to *think* like a farmer – and, I liked it. At every turn (and there were a LOT of turns), I saw contraptions. There were hay rakes that were 40 feet wide (That's a BIG hay rake). 20' tall combines that cut and sort corn to make my corn flakes. Sprayers, plows, and seeders of all types – and all designed, like a Transformer, to collapse into something you could drive on a road.

I gained a lot of respect for farmers that day. These guys were really *in* to this. They talked about tractors driving themselves and how their seed and fertilizer are the **best!** I was nonplussed. I don't even have seed.

We walked through an endless maze of enormous machinery. I saw an amazing robotic milking machine demonstration. We finally stopped for lunch at the Ohio cattlewomen's tent. Lunch conversation was dominated by an important realization by one of the nearby farmers. A $35,000 investment in a new sprayer could be amortized and paid off in 5 years.

These guys really knew what they were doing and I was out of my element. Throughout, Shar kept an even keel – knowing that the thrilling conclusion was coming – the Ohio State University Pawpaw patch!

There was such a blur of activity that we nearly missed our opportunity for the pawpaws. By the time we finally drove through the walnut harvest section on our tour, we didn't even get out of the hay ride to inspect the pawpaws. It made little difference as the highlight was perceived a little differently than expected.

There in the shade of a setting sun, we saw the Ohio State University patch. Frankly, even *I* was disappointed. Shar laughed as we passed noting that she had many pawpaws that were bigger and healthier than their plants. We then saw another patch planted in the sun – with some rather sad pawpaws eking out a living in Southern Ohio. *Everyone* knows you don't plant pawpaws in direct sunlight!

Shar was radiant. We'd come 500 miles to see this patch, but she had bigger, and healthier Pawpaws in our own back yard. I guess there is really no place like home.

Hall of Fame, Canton Ohio

This is the picture that I always dreamed about. As a high school football player I envisioned this moment when I would be at my induction ceremony into the Hall.

Shar met me (after my tour) and suggested that she, 'take a picture of you in front of that stupid old football place'. I don't think that's appropriate reverence.

On reflection, I wasn't that great of a football player ... and it looks like I'm wearing an enormous hat.

Chapter 5 - The Grand Farm Experiment

I think that one the most lovable things about Shar is the unexpected nature of what you'll find her involved with at any given time. She is always wrapped up in one pursuit or another and gets serious pleasure from everything that she does. It is a wonderful thing to hear her describe something that she likes doing and it really does inspire me sometimes to do the same thing. I don't usually have the same experience or joy she describes, but her enthusiasm is very infectious.

We lived in the relative security and comfort of suburbia for many years, but something was missing. One day she told me that the Home Owners Association had stopped by. There was apparently a strict covenant against food gardening in our neighborhood. The growing of tomatoes, corn, carrots and other vegetables is something my vegetarian wife enjoys and relies upon for food. Such a covenant might make sense in the front yard, but we both were perturbed that the rules extended to our back yard as well.

Of course she rebelled a bit. There were the 'volunteer' tomatoes that just grew next to our trees and shrubs. There were strawberries growing 'in the wild' in many places in the yard, but the days of rows of fresh veggies seemed to be passing her by. Of course, keeping chickens in your back yard meant that we always had a little extra scrutiny from the HOA.

Having grown up on various farms and in wooded areas, Shar had always wanted to return back to the country. She's always loved chickens, gardening and walking in nature so it was only natural (no pun intended) that she wanted to move to the country. So, like the Beverly Hillbillies in reverse, we purchased a farm and moved from the city to re-connect with our 'roots'.

Paradise Found

Two views of the barn on the property we purchased.
Beauty is in the eyes of the beholder!

As you might expect, not all of us had the same 'roots' as Shar and so there was a 'break-in' period. Having lived comfortably in AC and with electricity and running water in all of my previous homes, there was a little adjusting needed.

We dug a well, arranged for electricity at the site, and began planning for farm living. It was Green Acres all over again.

We sold our house to some suckers that didn't know about the vegetable laws or the chicken restrictions (should we have disclosed that?) and moved to our new dream property. We bought a tractor, and began our life as farmers - except that I would still commute to my regular job.

Trailer People Never Have a Nice Day

This quote, "trailer people never have a nice day," was originally told to me by a friend of mine in college describing his living conditions in a 30-year old mobile home. While I thought the quote was amusing at the time, I thought I'd forgotten it with the passing of time, but …

When we moved to the property, we needed a place to stay. We purchased a trailer from a nearby couple that had just completed building their country house. We were inspired by their tales of construction and country living and bought their trailer – a substantial step up from my college friend's hovel. The trailer was nice, with a bump-out in the back and a large open design.

Our Trailer

Nothing smells as nice as freshly weed-wacked hay in the front yard of your mobile home. There's no place like *this* home. We moved this trailer one time about ¼ mile without the assistance of any fancy trailer hitch or truck. Shar just used the bucket of the tractor to pull it! I can tell that story now that we've sold it and changed our insurance.

Even though the trailer came with all the amenities of comfortable living, unfortunately, the property lacked some. Without a proper septic system, we opted to use an outhouse. The outhouse needed to be near the road so that it could be serviced, leaving it about 100 yards from our trailer.

Now I wasn't an old man then, or at least not as old as I am now, but there's something about a hundred yard walk to the outhouse that really makes you consider that glass of water before bed. It didn't make a difference as I couldn't 'hold it' most nights and was forced to take an adventurous hike.

Most people today haven't really ever lived with an outhouse. I certainly had not. Still, it was always interesting to put on those flip-flops and take a walk. One night, I startled a deer who must have been within 10 feet of me. He snorted loudly to warn the others nearby that there was an intruder. I almost didn't make it to the outhouse that night.

Here's a quick 'day in the life' synopsis from those early days on the farm:

6:30 – Arrive home from work

6:35 – start big generator to charge batteries and pump water

6:40 – plug in trailer and pump to the well. Fill trailer's water reservoir.

6:50 – Turn off big generator, put cap back on water reservoir.

7:00 – Dinner

7:30 – Fish a little bit in the pond

7:32 – Catch first fish

8:00 – No more fish – Out to barn

8:05 – fix something in barn

8:55 – something half fixed – return to trailer

9:00 – start little generator for electricity to watch TV

9:30 – out of gas, read book

10:00 – lights out (literally – battery too drained)

2:00 AM – walk to outhouse in flip flops. Watch for wild animals.

All in all, trailer life was not too bad as long as you didn't forget something; like gas, starter fluid, extra batteries, spare parts for broken trailer things, etc. While I was busy with my duties, Shar kept herself busy with chickens.

The Egg Business

One of the great things about having a farm is that you can have as many chickens as you want. I'm sure a lot of you are saying, "That sounds too good to be true," and you would be right in that assessment. As it turns out, having over a hundred chickens is hard work.

Shortly after we moved to the property, I built Shar a chicken pen so that she could keep maybe a dozen chickens in an area near our barn. The pen was such a success that we built a second 'chicken tractor' near it. The chicken tractor is basically an open structure, constructed of chicken wire and horse fencing that houses perhaps 15-20 chickens and can be easily moved to allow the chickens to eat like free range while providing some cover.

She also bought some electric fencing and then more and more chickens until we had perhaps a half dozen chicken 'houses' of various types, and probably a quarter acre of fenced area that we rotated around near the barn. The open air, fresh grass, and good housing let the chickens thrive, and Shar continued to add to the flock.

At one point, we reached the peak of our chicken/egg laying business with about 125 chickens. Shar found a nearby health food store that sold the eggs and we were in business! The eggs came in a variety of shapes, colors and sizes, and the store could not keep them on the shelves. At $4.50 a dozen, the farm was now somewhat profitable as we were producing as many as 8 dozen eggs a day.

The Egg Laying Business – Production Side

Photo shows the chicken tractor at left with a variety of chicken houses, rest areas, day rooms, spas, office space, and egg laying locations. The compound is protected by an electric fence. What more could a chicken want?

Just about the time that it seemed that our business was taking off, we realized one important lesson about the egg laying business. Chickens are vulnerable to attacks from various animals. Some of the animals we had at the farm that liked to eat or kill chickens were: foxes, bears, dogs, coyotes, raccoons, snakes, hawks, owls, eagles, weasels, snapping turtles, young children, etc. Other than that, our chickens were completely safe.

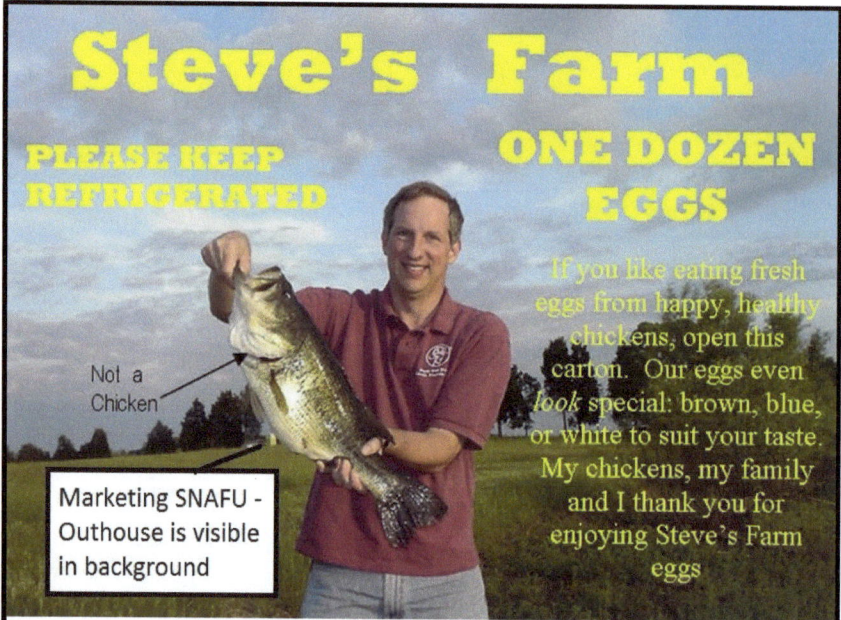

Steve's Farm

PLEASE KEEP REFRIGERATED

ONE DOZEN EGGS

If you like eating fresh eggs from happy, healthy chickens, open this carton. Our eggs even *look* special: brown, blue, or white to suit your taste. My chickens, my family and I thank you for enjoying Steve's Farm eggs

Not a Chicken

Marketing SNAFU - Outhouse is visible in background

The Egg Laying Business – Marketing Side

Photo shows one of the labels we made for our egg business. Important marketing lesson learned: Never underestimate the power of a handsome fish in selling eggs.

It wasn't long before we noticed that some of our chickens were disappearing. Sometimes we'd see the culprit in action, but mostly the attacks were carried out at night or when we weren't watching. We had inadvertently opened up the equivalent of a critter KFC.

Once the animals knew where the chickens were (and it was not hard for them to find), we had every varmint in the county eating the chickens, the eggs, or the chicken feed. One thing was apparent - we would not be in the business of feeding wildlife for very long, and once the cafeteria was open, we had visitors of every type. The electric fence is hard to maintain properly, and we had a real problem with birds of prey.

We posted a fake owl with a rotating head that worked for a bit. Shortly thereafter, we saw that we were losing about a bird a day to some new predator. We asked the neighbor what was killing the chickens in the unusual way we now saw. His answer, "looks like you've got an owl problem."

In the end, we had to scale the farm way back, giving many of our birds to a neighbor who had a more secure, if less wholesome, place for them to live.

Man Killer

The Eastern Red Cedar is a pretty tree and our property is fortunate to have some mighty specimens. The tree has a trademark smell that is highly desired in closets and drawers. The wood is a pretty red color and can be fashioned into comfortable, pleasant smelling furniture or flooring. It can also kill, but I'm getting ahead of myself.

When a large storm passed through our property one night we heard a thunderous crash and realized that we'd lost one of our big trees. It's always tough to see these majestic trees die, but this was a very big tree with a particularly unusual break. Lightning or a very large gust of wind had knocked the tree over with a small fragment of it connected to the stump about 7 feet off the ground. The balance of the tree fell into our neighbor's yard.

The tree was probably about 60 feet tall, and shortly thereafter I took on the job of cutting it up. It was not a trivial task. A neighbor drove by as I was working and said, "Looks like you've got a Man Killer there." I laughed the laugh of a man who was seriously re-thinking this tree removal project.

The peculiar break of the tree, which was probably almost 2 feet across where it severed, was a real problem. There was no good angle to cut the tree without the risk of it falling atop the cutter. My neighbor's words echoed in my head. I cut around the top of the tree, sawing off all the easy branches and working my way back to the stump. Every time I neared it, I became a little more unsettled. The tree was held to the stump by a 2-inch wide piece of wood across its base that was twisted and mangled. Would it hold if I cut off this branch? Or the next one?

Every time I cut a branch nearer the stump I'd hear a creaking noise like it might fall down and just crush my leg or pin my arm under its enormous trunk. But it was playing it cool – setting up to take me out completely. I studied my position. I was about to remark to Shar how dangerous this situation was when I turned to my side and saw this sight:

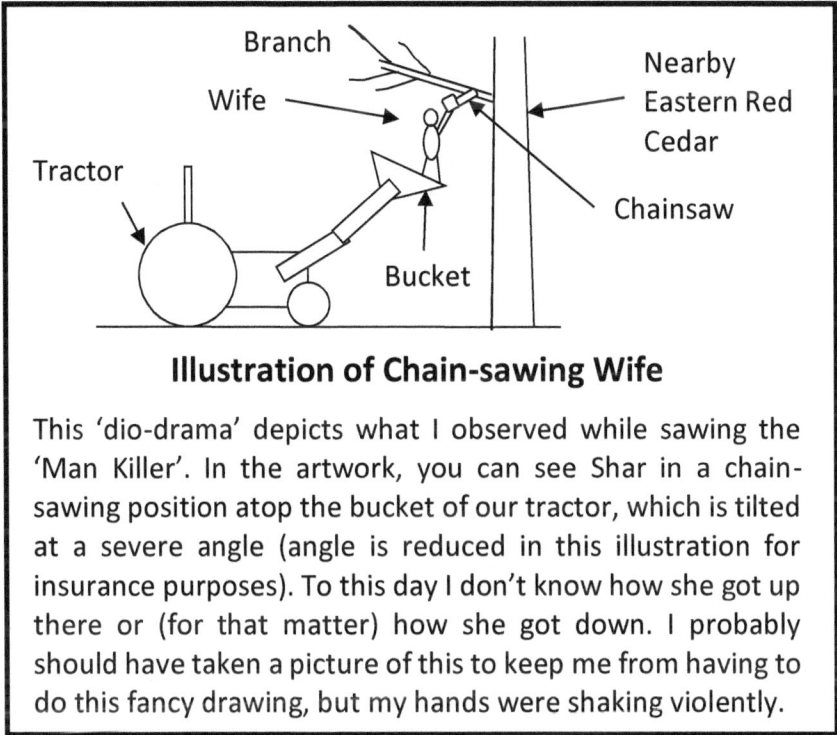

Illustration of Chain-sawing Wife

This 'dio-drama' depicts what I observed while sawing the 'Man Killer'. In the artwork, you can see Shar in a chain-sawing position atop the bucket of our tractor, which is tilted at a severe angle (angle is reduced in this illustration for insurance purposes). To this day I don't know how she got up there or (for that matter) how she got down. I probably should have taken a picture of this to keep me from having to do this fancy drawing, but my hands were shaking violently.

I decided to press on. Perhaps Shar was not the ideal partner to discuss dangerous situations. In order to reach the twisted piece of wood that were holding the body of the tree to the stump, I would need to stand directly under the trunk. This is not a favorable position when you consider that the tree trunk, when severed, usually falls downward.

I returned to trimming branches on the top of the tree (where the trunk was only a foot in diameter) and started to 'work my way back'. I was considering what kind of injury would be acceptable as a peace offering to this tree when I heard an enormous roar come over the hill.

Shar, secure in her Captain's chair on the tractor, lifted the bucket and with a low gear pushed the trunk of the tree at a strategic point about 6' in the air. With a thunderous 'CRACK', the Man Killer separated from its stump and the trunk fell to the ground with mighty thump.

59

I looked at my bride who had a wide smile. She would save my life many times, but that day she took down the Man Killer and I couldn't have been more proud of her. If you ever doubt if your spouse loves you, I'd suggest you take on an enormous task and get them on some heavy equipment. You might die, but you know, nothing says love like the crashing crunch of a loving spouse.

Merry Christmas

As anyone who has land will tell you, land use is important. On our property, we grow hay and sell it every year, but we also look for new and sometimes 'creative' ways to sell our farm products.

Shar was inspired by the sale of some of our redbud tree saplings to a friend of mine and decided to try her hand in the tree business. The only problem was, she didn't really have any marketable trees.

Absent a market, she made a market. After some slick negotiating (there may have been a pie involved), she sold her sister, Renee, a 'Christmas tree' for $40, sight unseen.

When I saw the tree, 'proudly' displayed in Renee's kitchen I laughed out loud. The 'Christmas tree' that Shar had picked out was a Spruce tree – probably 10' tall and no wider than 2' across. The tree looked like more of a 'Christmas toothpick' than a tree. Its top was bent over to fit in the kitchen, and tree skirt protruded out well beyond its branches.

I remarked that there wasn't any room under the tree for presents so this might not be a very good Christmas. Renee's husband had the best line. When an oak leaf fell out of the tree while we were 'admiring' it, he quipped, "Better put that leaf back in the tree before Shar figures out a way to charge us for it."

Fire Control Officer

The one constant on any farm with trees is that the trees will need to be cut, and will need to be burned. The work associated with trimming woods along a field will frequently result in some very large piles of branches, leaves, needles, logs, and giant trunks for burning. Once we had purchased the property, we compiled (over several months) several giant burn piles.

The first time we went to burn one of these piles was a bit of an overwhelming experience. The wood, much of it dry, included a lot of pine needles, leaves, and small branches which are super-combustible. We cut the hay around the wood and inspected the fire area. The grass was green but very dry, and I was about 90% sure the fire would not spread very much. We called the fire department to warn them (better start running now), and then set about burning our first two wood piles.

Armed with a shovel and a few gallons of water, Shar ran off to get the tractor, which would have a bucket-full of dirt for 'fire control'. I waited, and waited, and then decided to get things going, thinking - 'she'll be back shortly'. Besides, this brush pile was only about 20 feet across; what could happen?

The wood pile was remarkably combustible. Since the pile was so large, I lit three separate fires, one on each side of the pile. By the time I started the third fire, I could barely stand to be near the pile. Five minutes later, I was an outcast – 20 feet away, and shielding my face to keep it from igniting. I couldn't believe how hot this fire was.

On all sides, I saw the fire expanding out in a menacing fashion. The burning grass was radiating out in all directions at an alarming rate. I used the tools I had at my disposal, my feet, to run around the fire stomping out the farthest reaches of this 'ring of fire', but it kept getting bigger, and by now, the flames from this fire were probably 40-50' tall.

I ratcheted up my cussing, and stomping. Panic took over.

Shar will be back soon, I reasoned.

Inferno

When you see a fire this big burning this violently, your first thought is 'run for it'. 'Cooler' heads prevail, however, leading the fire's creator to run *toward* the fire, cussing, and alternately stomping the fire out of the grass, cinders, nearby animals, as well as boots, jeans, and his desire to own a farm. As with many farm dilemmas, the first thing on a farmer's mind is insurance coverage. This 'small' fire was handled correctly; standing back, watching with wide eyes and singed eyebrows.

Eventually, the ring of fire slowed its spread, and I realized that my name might not be on the front page of the paper. As I continued to stomp on any fire, I could see the flames receding. I looked on all sides for fires that may have been started by flying debris, and ran over to put a few of those out. Finally, the fire, now a comfy 10' tall, looked almost under control.

I took a deep breath and continued my praying. Rounding the corner, I saw Shar, just arriving with the tractor. She was oblivious to what had happened. She pulled up and asked how it was going. I told her that I had this fire under control, and suggested she start on the other wood pile, about 50 yards away. She walked over with a lighter and a good attitude.

I was torn about telling her how these fires burn. The devil on my left shoulder just laughed and said, "Don't help her!" Apparently the angel on my right shoulder had been burned off. She started burning her pile with predictably the same results I'd just experienced.

When her first screams started, I ignored her, saying 'I've got to control this one!' pointing at the 'campfire' I was not monitoring. This caused me and the devil to have a pretty good laugh. Eventually though, I ran over and helped tame her fire, which by this time had largely been stomped into submission by my poor, blackened wife.

Six hours later, when the fires had been put out, I asked Shar what had delayed her so much with the tractor. Apparently there were 'some nice rocks on the side of the road,' she'd picked up for a road repair. She had not even seen my mushroom cloud. Lesson learned – Always wait for your wife.

Chapter 6 -Daredevil

This section is devoted to the things that I've seen Shar do that I would consider dangerous. There are really so many things that I'm not sure where to start, but consider a few of these things that she's actually done recently:

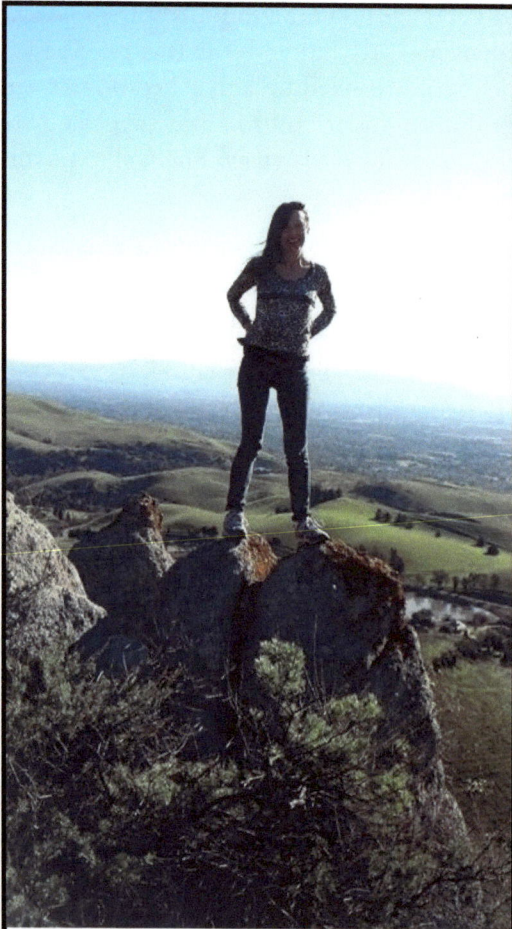

Daredevil
This is the type of stunt daredevils do, shortly before they fall to their death.

- For years she would jump up on the counters of our kitchen to reach high up into the upper reaches of the kitchen cabinets. She is not tall, so a certain amount of improvisation is necessary for someone who likes to cook as much as she does. But this would happen 4-6 times *per meal*. It was not unusual to see her, for example, walk over to one cabinet, jump up on the counter, reach for a bowl high in the cabinet, set it on the counter and then jump down. Then she might go over to the other side of the kitchen, jump up on the counter again, reach for a utensil in some out-of-the way location, put it on the counter, jump down again, etc. Thank goodness our new house has lower cabinets.

- One day, while we were walking around a golf course in Florida that I'd played on that day, I remarked about the size of an alligator I'd seen on one hole. When we reached that hole, there was that alligator – probably 10-12 feet long. She did not hesitate but walked *around the pond towards the alligator.* Mercifully, the alligator slithered into the water, probably to protect itself.

- While visiting Niagara Falls, Shar took a trail into the woods that emerged into the Niagara River. I trailed behind, keeping an eye on her. As I watched, she waded out into the river until I couldn't see her. When she returned, she only had this to say, "The current out there is really strong!" I'd get an insurance policy on her, but money can't replace that kind of bravado.

- When we first moved to the property I did a very foolish thing. While discussing the state of our pond, I mentioned that I could rent a bulldozer and probably do some of the work myself. It took me weeks of backtracking and outright lying that, "No, you cannot rent a bulldozer." Not that I worry about her and the bulldozer, it's just everything else that I'm concerned about. I believe you *can* rent a bulldozer, but I'm counting on her not reading this far into the book – and thus not discovering this 'nugget'.

Danger is My Game

Shar poses next to a sign warning about wading in the Niagara River a few hundred yards above the falls. Of course she waded in, describing the current as, "really strong"

- Shar enjoys aerial displays of daring. She has consistently maintained that any work on the roof of the house should be done only by her because, and I quote, "You don't have good balance." I would be very upset with her if I had better balance. Meanwhile, she's been on our roof and worked on the cupola in our barn a few times, usually suspended 20-40' above the ground on our rickety aluminum ladder. Did I mention that I have bad balance?

Chainsaws

If you saw the cover of this book, I think you'll recognize that my wife does not have a normal womanly relationship with chainsaws. Most of the women that I met before Shar actually had very few chainsaws. There was something about country living, however, that brought out her desire for dangerous equipment.

Last week, I mentioned to her family that she has six (6!) chainsaws. She quickly corrected me, however, "I only have 5; one is broken." I stand corrected.

In fairness, she can only operate about 4 of them (and only one or two at a time). She has an occasional 'farm hand' who provides many of the essential services at our property that can operate the other two. I believe that her friend, Hank, is in some ways the perfect helper for Shar. He has the following essential characteristics that I've identified as critical for working with my wife:

- Always willing to start slow, perhaps by having one of her nice, big, healthy breakfasts
- Patient, patient, more patient
- Strong, hard-working, capable of putting in long hours doing difficult, demanding physical labor
- Patient
- Puts tools away properly

Hank does all of these things, never complains, and is willing to work a full 12 hour day. Did I mention he was patient?

Chapter 7 - Risky Business

Cutting Neighborhood Waste

Shortly after we moved into our townhouse, we noticed a serious lack of parking. We complained, mostly to ourselves, for several months. We attended a Home Owners Association (HOA) board meeting to make a more formal complaint. As I recall, there were seven people in the meeting; the HOA Board, the property management rep, and us. I think that's pretty common. It would not stay that way, however.

After the first meeting, Shar decided that she would attend another meeting, this time without me (asking when it would be over). That night, she came home elated. She had been elected Secretary on the HOA board! The new position thrilled her and she was excited to get out and be involved in all of the critical issues of our community.

I love my wife. I love my wife, but she was not a good Secretary. The Secretary must take minutes and follow parliamentary procedure – recording the actions of the board for all posterity. The night before her second board meeting she came to me head-in-hands, at about 10 PM. "I'm supposed to write up minutes," was all she could say. One hour later, we (the team of Steve and Shar) had written up everything that she could remember, more or less. I did not want to show my work.

It made little difference as the other board members 'worked around' the bad minutes, frequently supplementing them after the meetings. The secretary position was really only a ruse, however. The primary objective was now in sight: Additional parking for our section of the neighborhood.

With the HOA board distracted by her minutes, Shar went into hyper-drive to get our parking at the top of the agenda. In her defense, our parking probably was in need of a serious upgrade. The county had recently removed some roadside parking, making our only other options an unsafe road crossing or a ¼ mile walk. Something needed to be done. What *was* done, however, was not something that will likely ever be repeated.

The HOA president, (I'll call him 'Tom') proposed a compromise. He mentioned that perhaps we could get the parking sooner, if we provided some 'sweat equity'. He noted some things that were in need of being done in the community. One item he mentioned was the removal of some pine trees that had recently suffered a blight.

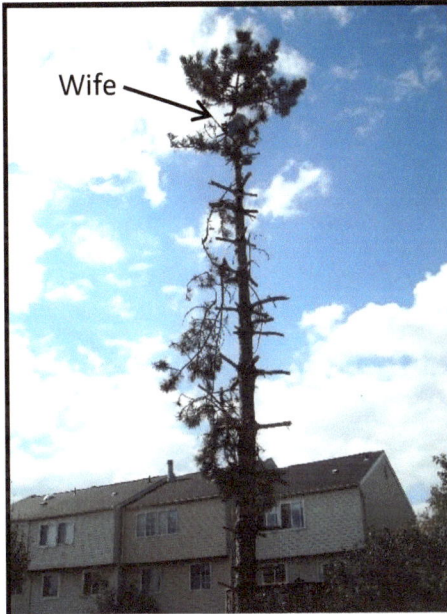

Wife

On Higher Ground

Here Shar takes down a blighted Pine tree threatening one of our neighbors. She works without a safety harness like all great freedom fighters. Thanks to our neighbor, Vic, who captured this pic of our hero in action during the Great Parking War of 2010. Viva la Parking!

Never mention the desire for tree removal to a girl with six chainsaws. Shortly thereafter, trees started going missing. Sometimes, I would help, sometimes our neighbor Vic would help. On weekends, or after work, we'd take down a tree or two each day. But mostly it was Shar, working every day. In one summer season, she personally, with very little help, removed over 70 trees. Big trees. Almost all of the trees were between 20 and 40 feet tall.

For each tree, she'd meticulously notch the tree, make it fall where desired, cut the branches, slice the tree into logs, and load all of it onto her truck. She'd make several runs to the dump, then come back, cut the stump down to ground level, and clean up all the small branches in the area.

By the end of the summer, she was ready to be paid.

Tom was a bit overwhelmed at the response. Perhaps he was blinded by the new sunlight now entering the neighborhood, but he did not offer any new parking. Instead, he did what all great HOA Presidents do: He took it under advisement.

To say that Shar was displeased would be understating it a bit. The situation came to a head when another woman in the neighborhood came to the HOA meeting with her request. She wanted streetlights for her, 'extra parking.'

This was war. "How dare she ask for lights for extra parking?! We don't even have *any* extra parking!" Shar exclaimed. Flyers were distributed. Torches were lit. Pitchforks were sharpened. The battle was afoot!

The next board meeting had the highest attendance on record. At the board were the HOA board members (including Shar), 30 neighbors (all from our street), and one visibly shaken, highly pregnant woman who just wanted streetlights for her extra parking.

The pre-meeting gathering said it all. Tom, a tall, healthy police officer, attempted to control what can only be described as a mob. In desperation, he yelled what all great HOA Presidents yell: "Your parking is not on the agenda!" The crush was too great, and he finally relented to allowing everyone into the packed meeting room.

The agenda was disrupted as the mob shouted parking chants. The pregnant woman wanting streetlights only handed in her signatures, not uttering a word. After consultation with the Property Management representative (who was looking out for the safety of his board room), Tom finally allowed each person to speak for 1 minute.

The neighbors provided unspeakable parking horrors. Our pregnant mother (sure, we had one too) told of rushing her kids across a busy dark street after parking in another neighborhood. I told of walking 1/3 mile in 18" of snow to where my car was parked. One brave man had nearly frozen to death looking for a space. The tide was officially turned.

Today, largely as a result of my lovely wife, we have 36 new parking spaces. She is a hero in this neighborhood, universally loved (well, there's always *one* neighbor) and revered. We will not soon forget, however, the Great Parking War of 2010.

Green Eyed Monster

One day I found out why Shar buys her chainsaws and maintains them at a shop in nearby Leesburg, Virginia. His name is Tommy. When I first heard about Tommy, the green-eyed monster of jealousy appeared. She spoke in such glowing terms: "Tommy is so nice," "Tommy can fix anything," "Tommy always … blah, blah, blah …" I am not usually the jealous type, so I was surprised when Shar invited me to meet Tommy one day when we were engaged in a day of putting in long hours doing difficult, demanding physical labor.

"We need to go to Leesburg," she said. "Tommy fixed one of my chainsaws and we'll need it so we can both work on that tree." And so, it was on.

I was not at my best. I'd spent 6 hours chain-sawing and dragging trees and stumps to a central place for burning. I was spent. Still, the idea of meeting Tommy intrigued me, and I could use the rest. What was it about him that kept Shar coming back?

In my mind, I imagined Tommy as an Adonis; a perfectly sculpted Greek God. He was also witty, charming, and capable of fixing small engines. I sneered as only a jealous husband can sneer. I also resolved to learn more about small engine repair.

As we drove to Leesburg, I imagined myself standing tall (probably with twigs still sticking out of my hair) and facing Tommy head on. I think Shar sensed that I was a bit intimidated about meeting Tommy, so she consoled me. "Have you met Tommy before?" she asked, a smile on her face. I admitted that I had not.

"Well, you'll like him," she teased. There was a dramatic pause. Then, there was another dramatic pause. "He kind of looks like the Bob's Big Boy statue," she admitted – a growing grin on her face.

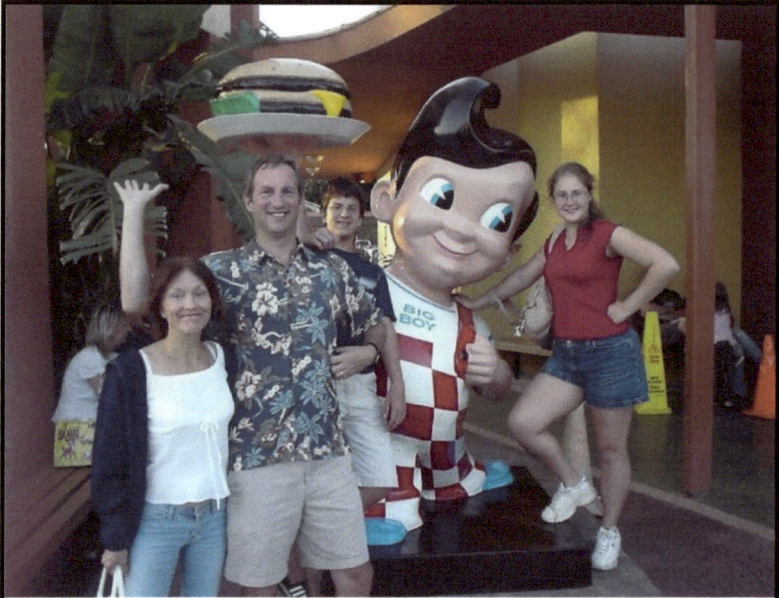

"Tommy" – Posing with Family

Here we see the family with the Big Boy statue (AKA: Tommy). In the photo I laugh the laugh of a man making fun of his nemesis (although this picture was taken before I'd actually met Tommy). I'm keeping Tommy away from my wife, but wait! – Is he making eyes at my daughter?!? Apparently I'd better keep a close watch on this Tommy character ...

I recoiled at the thought. Was he also delicious? Then coolness returned. I imagined the statue in question. A short, rotund young man with a burger tray held high in his hand. I felt immediately relieved. Perhaps I could postpone my small engine repair studies.

The delivered goods were as promised. Tommy was witty, charming, short, rotund, and capable of delivering an awesome burger (I suppose). Sure enough, he delivered the repaired chainsaw and even had some words of advice about how *I* could repair it myself. Was I just imagining the smell of French fries?

One More Pawpaw Story

It would be a shame to leave out of this fine book the contribution my wife has made to pawpaw production in America. As I mentioned in my Farm Science Review, the pawpaw is a native fruit that grows well in the eastern US. It's also Shar's favorite obsession. It would not be an understatement to say that she is the 'Johnny Appleseed' of pawpaws.

I don't think anyone who knows Shar would say that her devotion to this fruit is anything less than an obsession. Over the last 6 or 8 years, she has attended several pawpaw conventions, and single-handedly introduced several hundred plants to … wherever she can put them. Each of these trees, which are very hard to grow, is lovingly tended, watered, and coddled into a healthy, pawpaw producing tree.

In the late Fall, on a good year, she will harvest a few dozen pawpaws, proudly displaying them and sharing them with friends and neighbors. The fruit, to me, tastes a little like a banana. A big pawpaw is not much bigger than your fist, and has a large seed inside it. Personally, I'm not a big fan of the pawpaw, but I am an enormous fan of its number one cheerleader.

Say I put a blindfold on, and started walking in the woods behind my house. In any direction, at any distance within a half mile, I could pull off that blindfold and look down and likely see the following:

- A tomato cage with a pawpaw growing within it
- The pawpaw will have rocks around its base to deter weeds
- The pawpaw tree will be healthy, if not small, but free from the normal travails of weeds or nearby trees – due to careful tending

I have seen Shar take down a 30' tree to allow some additional sunlight to fall on a favorite pawpaw tree in one of her patches. It is also not unusual for her to gather pollen from some pawpaw trees and pollinate buds on another tree to ensure that she has fruit in the fall.

American Pawpaws
These squishy, banana-like fruits grow in the Eastern US. They are also Shar's obsession. I think it's because Shar and the plants both enjoy being in the woods, being near streams and in the shade.

Shortly after we moved to our current house she was excited to report to me that she'd found, "a secret pawpaw patch." She went to great lengths to report the size of the trees and the sheer numbers of pawpaw trees growing in this location. One day, after making me swear secrecy, she took me to her special place in the woods. I found it all particularly charming.

You might say that the nurturing of pawpaw trees is an odd obsession, and you would be correct. But for my wife it is just the right obsession. It allows her to be in the woods – which she loves. She keeps healthy by planting and tending the trees in nature. The plants thrive near stream beds. Shar thrives near stream beds. For her, the trees give her peace and purpose, which is all that any of us really search for.

I have grown to love pawpaws because I love her, and fortunately, I too am her obsession.

Chapter 8 - Snakes

I can't believe I've gone this far in the book without discussing Shar's relationship with snakes. I've never liked snakes and I think most people agree with me that they are 'icky', for lack of a better term; and then there's Shar.

Snakes!

Shar has always loved snakes. In this section you will see that she is smiling in all the pictures. She is really at her best when she's enjoying nature, and she enjoys it most when she can experience it up close, touching it and feeling it (note turtle in foreground). Some people might not agree, but I've come around to her thinking. Snakes have an important part to play in this world, too. Just please not near me!

When I first met Shar she was the apartment manager at the small apartment complex where I lived. At the time, I had no money and plenty of free time at night so she would give me odd jobs, paying me with quarters from the vending machines. I did not realize that she was my wife-to-be, but there was a fascination from the beginning.

Take the time we were in the basement of building 3. We were moving a sofa in the basement when a huge blacksnake slithered out as I lifted the sofa. My first reaction was to jump, then to get to higher ground, then decide how I might kill it without hurting myself.

Shar just looked at me.

"He lives here," she said. Apparently that explained it.

We moved the sofa.

Beautiful

This is one of my favorite pictures of Shar. If you overlook the fact that she's holding a giant slug on a rock, you'll see that Shar is really very pretty. In her eyes it's really the slug that's beautiful – which is really lovely; particularly if you don't find slugs disgusting.

She later explained that the snake kept the mice from coming in and that she and the snake had an 'understanding', which apparently I lacked.

I will give her this, however, she has always been a steadfast advocate for snakes. She likes bats (they eat flies), lizards (more flies), and other crawly things as well – including many of the things most of us do not enjoy. To be honest, I'm afraid to ask her opinion on mosquitos.

Our neighbor once mentioned that she'd seen a large blacksnake living in a hole under her front steps. My thoughts immediately turned to whether this was a 'refugee' snake that Shar had rescued from some other place. It was not. It was merely a 'free spirit' that had apparently 'lost his way'. Our neighbor, who regularly jumped a few steps 'just in case' was not as sympathetic. Shar made a deal with her that if she saw it again, she should call us and we would 'take care of it'. I think her approach and mine might have differed if I was the 'we' in that scenario.

Anyway, we have always had a hard time getting to church on time. One morning things were going especially slow and I was rushing Shar out of the house when the phone rang. It was the neighbor; the menace snake was lurking under her steps. Shar sprang in to action. She ran to the neighbor's house. There was the culprit, coiled at the base of the steps.

Perhaps you've seen the now defunct show, "Crocodile Hunter." In that show, the late Steve Irwin would entertain us weekly with his expertise in the handling of a variety of frightening wild animals. Part of the show's attraction was his ludicrous disregard for personal safety in showing us one 'beauty' after another. One of his specialties was snake handling, a skill he had mastered through years of practice.

Few people understand correct snake handling protocol, but I am married to one who does. She made an overture to distract the snake, and then used her back hand to quickly grab it behind its head. She posed for a picture with the neighbor's son, and then put the snake into a bag for later transport to our farm. We made it to church on time.

Crikey, She's a Beaut!
Here Shar poses with our neighbor's son after she's extracted this snake from under their steps. I thought the gloves were a nice touch, but she usually doesn't bother. She wanted to have the boy hold the snake, but he declined. Notice he's packing heat just in case.

I can't tell you how many times since I've known her that she has found a snake, placed a snake in a safe place, recovered a snake from a dangerous place, or just played with a snake she found. If I had a picture of every snake that she's found or handled I could probably fill this book, but then, the first impulse I have is not to get a camera when I see a snake. If you ask yourself how many pictures you have of your wife holding a snake you'll see that Shar is very special, but particularly special to this husband.

One final story about Shar and snakes. Shar is smart enough to know that a blacksnake is not poisonous, and she (probably) would not go after a rattlesnake in the same way. Several years ago, however, I was working in New Mexico on business and Shar was visiting. She wandered into several nearby parks and, of course, wandered off the trail a bit. As she was walking, she found herself face-to-face with a large rattlesnake. She backed off and phoned me at work.

I could tell she was flustered, and frightened. As she related the story, I asked, "How big was the snake?" She thought about it a bit, still shaken up, and responded after a bit, "It was … it was … it was as big as a stick!"

We all had a pretty good laugh at that one once she recovered.

Epilogue

I hope you have enjoyed these stories about Shar. This epilogue tells one more story; the story of how we met.

Many people have wonderful stories about spying their future spouse from across the room. Others tell how they were so nervous they spilled something, tripped, stuttered or otherwise botched a simple introduction. I think we can all relate to these things, but this is not how it happened for me. But let me not get ahead of myself.

So much of this book is about the joy and adventure of marriage, but it has not always been that way for me. I will warn you now that God plays an important part in my life, and an important part in this story as well. If you are an atheist or an agnostic, read ahead at your own risk – but I know what happened.

I hope that as you read this you are with someone that you love. Your spouse may not be as perfect as Shar, but if you have love that is all that matters. A big part of why I wrote this book is to express my appreciation for her. She entertains me, cares for me, and has a deep concern for me. She is not perfect, but she is perfect for me. And that's why this story must be told.

Things were not always this good for me. In the late 1990's I was in the midst of a very difficult divorce. Divorce is never good, and this was no exception. There is a great deal of pain in divorce. The guilt of going through something this horrific wears on you like a heavy weight on your chest. Worse yet, I had kids by my ex-wife and I knew that separation from them would be hard on all of us. You can't underestimate how difficult and emotionally wasting that feeling is.

Our house had been sold, and I needed to search for a place to live. To make matters worse, I had almost no money. There was very little hope in my heart and I was emotionally exhausted.

Please, please, please – if you are having difficulty with your spouse work to get your differences settled. Many circumstances may seem problematic, but you will have no greater problem than when you go through a divorce.

At that time, religion had a very small part in my life. I'd grown up Catholic, but 'lost my religion' over the years. On that day, however, as I drove to look for a new place to live, I felt impressed to pray.

I don't know much about God, but I do know that he has helped me many times when things were not going right in my life. In this particular instance, I prayed again. I didn't know what to pray for, but I felt convicted that I should never go through this in my life again. I pulled off to the side of the road. I prayed that this would never happen to me again. I prayed that if I ever *did* get married again, that He, God, would choose who I should marry.

Satisfied that I had made peace, I drove from my house to nearby Fairfax City to look for an apartment. I had lived in a very low-cost apartment complex before and decided to head there as a first option for a new place. As luck would have it, I'd gone only a few miles when I saw a sign for an apartment for rent right in Fairfax City. I circled back and drove into the complex – which consisted of three old apartment buildings on a large lot.

The buildings looked serviceable (and low cost), and I found that there was a playground at the nursing home next door. I looked for the office, but could not find it. I called the number on the sign, left a message saying I was interested in the apartment, and drove away.

At this point, let me alter the story to tell Shar's side of the story. One of the advantages of being married for a while and telling this story many times together is that I've heard her side so many times that I can tell it just like her – but with a deeper voice.

At that time, Shar was the apartment manager at the building that I had just visited. As she's told me many times since then, when she first heard my voice, she was strongly impressed that 'this is the man you will marry'. Unfortunately, the voice did not take into account that the apartment had just been rented. Shar says that she was upset because, as she told the voice, "Well, I guess I'll just have to call my 'future husband' and tell him that the apartment is rented." It's better when she tells it because she has a very sarcastic tone.

81

Anyway, I did not like any of my other housing options. When she called later to tell me that there was no vacancy, I was not deterred. In fact, I was desperate. None of the other options was working out, and I had to move within a few weeks. I asked if I could see the apartment anyway in case another one came open. She agreed to show me the open unit since the renter had not yet moved in.

And so it started. I would be lying if I said that it was love at first sight. As I stated before, it was desperation at first. I thought she was attractive, but I was an emotional wreck. I didn't need a girlfriend or a wife or even a friend who was a girl - I needed an apartment.

I liked the apartment and told her to call me if anything opened up. As a follow up question I asked about my nearby neighbors on the third floor of the apartment building. After an in-depth description of the others on that floor, she casually mentioned that she was the neighbor in the apartment next door. I was intrigued (she was cute, and had very pretty blue eyes), but still, mostly, just desperate.

Then I left – taking my 'future husband' contingent apartment applications and driving off.

What happened next neither of us expected. When the day came for the other renter to move in, he did not move in. Shar called him repeatedly, but there was no answer. The mystery renter had dropped off the face of the earth. Shar called to return his cash deposit, but there was no answer.

I got the call that the apartment was available as I was finalizing my plans to move back in with my parents. I drove over, signed the application and a check, and moved in the next weekend.

Now a good love story would have us blossom into a true romance over the weeks and months after we'd first met – but this is not a good love story. Sorry about that.

Shortly after I'd moved in, my kids started to play with her son, who was at a convenient age in the middle of my kids. As the apartment manager, Shar had many responsibilities, several of which required long hours of physically demanding work. Since I was a pauper, we worked a deal where I would do odd jobs for her with my pay coming from the laundry room quarters. I jingled quite a bit in those days.

As Shar tells it, she used some of her feminine wiles in those first few weeks and months to show interest, but I was not receptive. In fairness, I was still a wreck. Besides, Shar was a vegetarian and I was a 'meat and potatoes' man. Nothing good could come from a union like that, I thought.

But then Shar presented a constant barrage of soups, lovingly prepared and arriving at the last minute – just as I was preparing to microwave my frozen pizza. At first, I would thank her, take the soup, and eat it in my lonely apartment. It was pitiful really.

I should state here that I am not the type of man that can take care of himself. Sure, I can handle myself in a knife fight or a dark alley, but I've always made a mess of the domestic aspects of life. I don't like to vacuum and I would describe my old apartment charitably as 'dusty'. I was wrecking about one dress shirt a week in the washing machine and my diet was atrocious. Perhaps the only nutrition that was keeping me alive was coming from this steady supply of soup from next door.

Months went by. I wouldn't characterize my attitude at that time as 'playing hard to get', but rather as 'oblivious'. I continued to observe my boss 'in the wild' however, and begin to notice that she was different than the other women I'd met.

As time went on I started inviting her over to help me eat her soup, and that was the beginning of the end for my bachelor life. In fairness, I can't say that I miss it much. I had one plant that I cared for that was named 'Thirsty'. I think that about says it all about my domestic life.

We grew a garden together (ok, *she* grew a garden while I watched and threw seeds out periodically). We went to museums with the kids, and her son Caleb went with my kids on our periodic walks.

Love started to blossom, and I really grew to like her. "Could this be the one?" I thought. But I would quickly disavow that possibility as I sat down to eat a big, satisfying steak dinner (carryout).

Eventually, though, I realized that I was no match for this power-packed girl who loved me more than I loved myself.

Shar has a deep and abiding faith in God that I admire greatly. I wouldn't say that I followed her example in that way initially, but I did find it to be a big source of the peace that she had, and that she shared with me. When I was with her I felt that things were going to be alright, and I still feel that way. I often catch myself smiling when I see her walking in a store or down the street. She has an encouraging air with me.

She's often said I would be a great doctor, radio commentator, politician, sports announcer or any other position that a person might aspire to. I personally don't believe that to be the case, but it shows why I love her. She doesn't think that I would be good at these things, she actually *believes* that's the case.

I often tell people that I meet in church an axiom that I believe: There is no greater power in the universe than the love of a godly woman.

I didn't understand that then, but I finally determined that this was what made her different than the other women that I'd met. Oh, and the soup – that was good soup. Today I call that 'marriage soup' because I always ask for it when I'm feeling down, tired, depressed or malnourished. It always satisfies and I know that it is filled with healthful veggies and love.

Months turned to years and I realized that my prayers had been answered. My diet was atrocious and I recognized that perhaps some vegetarian food would help keep me alive longer. I reasoned that if God kept putting her right in front of me, why didn't I marry her already?

Finally, she told me one day that she was moving. *Moving?!?*

She had purchased a house about five miles away. She and Caleb would be leaving in a few weeks and that was it.

In fairness, I was planning to move as well – so it was settled, sorta.

And then we were apart. I slipped back into my self-destructive ways, and watched the dust accumulate. I missed her, but was too full of pride to admit it and call her. So I waited, watched TV, and missed that soup.

One day, she called to ask if she could have her son's bike back. I'd completely forgotten that I even *had* the bike and told her that I'd bring it over. I was VERY glad that she'd called and it was not long before we were seeing each other regularly again. It was a very happy time for both of us.

I resolved during that time to ask her to marry me, and 'waited for a sign'. The problem with the 'waiting for a sign' method is that a sign is pretty much necessary, and they don't come around often. It's also hard to explain to your spouse-to-be why you're dragging your feet so much. The bar for a 'sign' started to drop – but still no action.

Finally, one night, while we were sitting alone in her house with the lights off on the sofa, I noticed that the moonlight from a high window in her living room was illuminating our faces. I jumped at the chance!

A few months later we were married by a justice of the peace, one day after my parent's 40th anniversary. At least I will not have to worry about forgetting my anniversary. We went to the movies for our honeymoon, and then I went to work the next day. Just remember, that's how things work when you're waiting for a sign.

Today, I sit here married for 18 years. I have created many memories with Shar that I treasure, and I am grateful to God for his answer to my prayers - giving me the wife that He would have me marry. May you be blessed in life to find such a love.

The End

APPENDIX A
SuperWife Song

When I first was married I was in the habit of calling Shar my 'SuperWife'. Over the years, I've called her this off and on, but finally committed this song to her as a love ballad, sorta.

The music is meant to be sung with a southern gospel twang, and a two part harmony. The melody is way too complicated to explain. Here's the Lyrics to SuperWife:

Some wives are Goooood,

    some wives are better

Some wives are greaaaat,

    that's better too

She rocks my woooorld,

    There's only one word to describe it

she's a

    SuperWife

    SuperWife

    Built to protect my life

    SuperWife

    SuperWife

    The keeper of my destiny

    SuperWife

    SuperWife

    I'll tell you more later ...

    SuperWife!

    SuperWife!

Trophy can't describe it

Goood-to-greaaaat-to-SuperWife!
    Put her on a pedestal
Goood-to-greaaaat-to-SuperWife!
    she's not that tall
Goood-to-greaaaat-to-SuperWife!
    Never mind she'll
Goood-to-greaaaat-to-SuperWife!
    ... get up there herself

she's powerful ...
I hear she heals biiiiirrrds
    (and I hear snakes too!)
She's POWER Packed!
    and she's all mine

(Guitar solo)   she's an angel
        (*she's a nature ranger!*)
    half my size,
        (*but twice my danger*)
A perfect doooooll,
    (lean and clean)
A gift from Gooood,
    (*read the testimony*)

And what about ... housework - she's amazing
Cooks and cleans (*I live like a king!*),
Fresh bread and clean sheets,
And veggie soup if that's your thing.

She's arranging socks ...- it's impressive - (here birds chirp)
sorted in rows in two different ways
I'm a living king - bountifully blessed
with working hands, she's the best

she's awesome ...

   (what do you call it? whaddaya call it?)
she's a

    SuperWife!

    SuperWife!

    Built to protect my life

    SuperWife!

    SuperWife!

    my living saavioor

    SuperWife!

    SuperWife!

    Part wildlife, part circus

    SuperWife!

    SuperWife!

(Wind doooooowwwwn)

She's a dynamo

She's a lady

    she's funner to watch than TV

watch her work now

she's got it going

    she's better than me

(fade out to another chorus of uptempo superwife)

she's a

SuperWife!

SuperWife!

The love of my life

SuperWife!

SuperWife!

my living saavioor

SuperWife!

SuperWife!

Part wildlife, part circus

SuperWife!

SuperWife!

APPENDIX B
Marriage Soup Recipe

When Shar read this book, she was very appreciative. She insisted, however, on a few critical changes. One of those changes is provided here – her recipe for Marriage soup. If you have a half hour, some ingredients and someone you love (or are just interested in), you might make a batch. If your friend is malnourished, all the better. The secret ingredient is love.

Ingredients:

2 cans Progresso Tomato Basil soup

1 can V-8 juice (12 oz.)

Tomatoes (pureed or sauce) (14 oz.)

½ package frozen greens (spinach or kale)

2 zucchini (or small yellow squash), sliced and quartered

1 whole onion, chopped

1 can organic kidney beans

1 cube vegetarian bouillon

Cook until zucchini is done, adding onion and beans last (so that the onions still have some crunch).

Enjoy!

www.ingramcontent.com/pod-product-compliance
Lightning Source LLC
Chambersburg PA
CBHW041214270326
41930CB00001B/10